Uncertainty to Confidence

Uncertainty
to
CONFIDENCE

A New Way of Living Your Life

Karissa Thomas

New You Publishing Incorporated

Uncertainty to Confidence: A New Way of Living Your Life

Visit our website at www.newyoupublishing.org.

Library of Congress Control Number: 2010922214

Cover, interior design, and typesetting: Glenna Collett
Editor: Jo-Ann Langseth
Author stylist & photographer: © GoGlamBeauty

ISBN 978-0-615-34538-3

Printed in the United States of America.

I dedicate this book in memory of Theresa Sookan (1925–2000), my beloved grandmother, mentor, and friend. She was always moved by my writing. I wrote her letters to make her happy, and she cried tears of joy every time. She encouraged and inspired my natural talent for sharing messages, and she taught me how to write from the heart. She inspired me to be a writer. Even today, I write for her.

We Wear the Mask

We wear the mask that grins and lies,
It hides our cheeks and shades our eyes,—
This debt we pay to human guile;
With torn and bleeding hearts we smile,
And mouth with myriad subtleties.

Why should the world be over-wise,
In counting all our tears and sighs?
Nay, let them only see us, while
        We wear the mask.

We smile, but, O great Christ, our cries
To thee from tortured souls arise.
We sing, but oh the clay is vile
Beneath our feet, and long the mile;
But let the world dream otherwise,
        We wear the mask!

Paul Laurence Dunbar (1872–1906)

Contents

Foreword xiii
Preface xvii
Acknowledgments xxv

Introduction 1

1 Life Unfolding 11

The Lessons 12
The Signs 14
Confronting Ourselves 15
You're ready for the flow 16
The flow of joy 17
The flow of balance 18
The flow of Consciousness 19
The flow of love/spirit 20

2 Life Experiences 23

Resentment 24
Healthy vs. Unhealthy Relationship 25
Marriage and You 26
Friends and You 27
Adversity 28
Self Honesty 30
Change 33
Dishonesty 33

The In-Between 35
Life Experiences and Their Connection to Source 36
Listen to Source 37
Back to Source 39

3 Consciousness Power, Control, Manipulation and Courage 41

Life's Bullies 41
Control 43
Your Personal IGPS (Internal Guidance Positioning System) 44
Vulnerability 45
Level of Consciousness 46
The Crazy 47

4 The Keys 49

Key of Time 49
Key of Inspiration 50
The Key of Silence 50
Self-Honesty 51
Happiness 51
Self-Reflection 52
Inspiration 53
People 54
Spirituality 56
Pray 56
Giving 58
Consciousness 59
Asking 61
Asking and Not Receiving 64

5 The Power within the Self 69

The Mind 70
Unknown 71
Life's Design 72
Ego 73
Disconnect 75
Turn Around 76
Judging Others 76
Insecurity within the Self 77

6 Clarity 79

Self-Talk 81
Unreality 83

7 How Special Am I? 87

Physical Self 88
Confession 89
You Are Special 89
Internal Self 90
We are All Special 91
Energy 91
Reinforce Goodness 93
The Magnitude of Energy 94
Where Do I Fit In? 95

8 What Should I Be Doing Now? Life Map 97

Disconnection along the Way 99
Spirit 100
Positive Attitude 100
The Goal 103

Cleansing Mentally 103
Cleansing Physically 104
Cleansing Environmentally 105
Moving on in My Life 106
Acceptance of People 107

9 Why Am I Here? 109

10 Who Am I? 115

Marriage 116
Selflessness 117
Disconnection in a Relationship 118

11 What's Next? 123

12 What Am I Not Getting? 127

13 If I Could Do It Over 133

14 Accepting Where I Am 139

15 Did My Mission to Earth Succeed? 147

Mission to Mars 148
Life 150

16 Here for Me and Not for You 153

Epilogue 156

Foreword

Kathleen Thomas

I am honored and delighted that my daughter has asked me to write the foreword to this book. Every parent always has something nice to say about their child regardless of their child's achievements—or lack of them. However, I must say that I am inspired and blessed to have the kind of child that I do. She has the heart of a humanitarian and the soul of a leader. She is driven, passionate, and committed to following her heart. It is through her that I was able to find the courage to keep moving forward. It was because of her that I kept in the struggle and did not fall by the wayside. I have lived my life for her so that she can have everything my mother couldn't afford for me and my nine brothers and sisters.

She is my one and only child, and, as every parent would hope and wish, she's turned out to be ambitious, motivated, and in the loving presence of good company. My mother always told me that she wasn't afraid for me. I was always upset hearing her say this, but now, as her soul is at peace and has moved on from this Earth, I can say that I understand what she meant. I can say that I am not worried for my daughter. My daughter is a go-getter. She has the strength of a lion and the perseverance of a blind man.

It is true that a parent, a teacher, a believer can see the potential of someone at a distance. What I can see for others sometimes others can't see for themselves. Even when I won the Miss

Trinidad and Tobago queen show, I didn't see what others saw in me. They saw a beautiful girl; they saw a talented, humble individual, but all I knew was that I was young, and inexperienced. I loved music and wanted to do well for my mother because she had worked so hard to make sure we were always happy at home.

As an experienced, mature woman, I can now say with conviction that I am a woman with a mission. I've had my fair share of life experiences that have made me the person I am today. I am able to recognize when someone is trying to take advantage of me. I am able to recognize when people aren't being genuine and kind toward me. People are always trying to get in my way of success. I am able to see this world for what it is and to see people for who they are.

For some strange reason, people always think I am someone that I am not. People's impressions of me are far from the truth of who I really am. This is a truth I've come to understand—that people always assume they know about your life and about your struggles, but they truly don't know anything—and so much of nothing. Many people have tried to prevent me from attaining the success that the universe has already bequeathed me. But I am from wellsprings of abundance, and people can't prevent me from getting what is already mine.

I am a woman, a mother, a friend, a teacher, a student, a driver, a driver of my life. When life calls for me to play the game of life, I play. When life asks me to listen, I listen. When life asks me to be humble and take nothing for granted, I obey.

I don't know where my strength comes from, but I am happy that I have the drive and intelligence to maneuver through this life. Looking back on my life, I can see that I didn't understand a lot of things that I do now. I probably wouldn't have wasted as much time with people and situations that weren't getting me anywhere. I probably would have spoken up for myself instead of allowing people to get the best of me. I probably would have changed my circle of friends.

I definitely would have wanted my mother to experience more of this world than she was able to. I would have wanted my father to have the luxuries and ease that life offers to all of us. As I get older and people are dying—my friend from cancer, my sister in a car accident, and my brother from complications after surgery—life is so much more precious to me.

I value the time I have with my family. I cherish the moments I have with my friends. I love seeing my daughter grow up to be a great woman. Her message would have saved me so much time! It would have brought clarity to me when I was struggling toward understanding. Although her message still inspires me and keeps me on my toes and on mission for what I am here to do, I still wish someone had spoken these words in my ears when I was growing up.

Who would have ever thought that the child would have instruction for the parent? Life is funny that way. Our teachers in life come in all different forms. While I am my daughter's mother and can still give her guidance, she is the voice of reason I wish I had many years ago.

She continues to inspire me daily. I am not afraid to confide in her my fears and even my dreams because she is so clearly a mouthpiece for Source, and capable of shaping and changing my life although I am the parent.

I know this book will inspire in many the hope that they need to come more into themselves. I know it has done so for me. I have spent years earning two master's degrees, and I have worked in the Board of Education system for ten years as a teacher, and as a dean. Throughout, I've seen families and people who could really use this message to check in with themselves.

So many of us are searching, and so many of us will continue to search for the remainder of our days here on Earth. Here's hoping that they find this book and begin to understand the design of life and the meaningful roles they must play in this life. May this book find you well, and impact your life in far-reaching ways.

Preface

In my continuing effort to understand life and my relationship to its design, this book was formed. In searching for the answers to my existence, I discovered that my understanding of life is very much a part of my well-being. Life had already given me all I needed to make sense of this existence in my mind, body, and soul. It is through these instruments that I am forever connected to Source. Life has given all of us these tools of understanding through our unlimited mental and spiritual connection to divinity. It is through that mental and spiritual connection that clarity is born and our existence understood.

Knowledge and wisdom are gained from life experiences, from the beginning of life to its end. They are the propellers in our lives, preventing us from being stationary and stagnant beings. Knowledge and wisdom keep us growing and fulfilling our destinies. It is through our spiritual connection to life that happiness, joy, and well-being are obtained. It is through our soul connection to the spirit world that life and our participation in this world come to fruition.

It wasn't until I started writing this book that this profound understanding of what life truly means started to make sense to me. I always had thoughts about my existence, but they were just thoughts, thoughts that stayed in my head. I started to write down my experiences as a way of comprehending what was transpiring in my life, and as a result I opened myself to direct connection to Source.

In writing down my experiences, I was able to analyze the text, and spirit resonated. It was through this resurrection of consciousness and spirit that I was able to discover my purpose. Had I not written down my experiences, I probably would still have confusion going through my head about life and its meaning, but I don't think that was life's plan for me.

After all, it's been said to me by my friends and family that 'things happen in your life for a reason.' My life happened the way it did so that I could be here in this moment, writing this book. I don't think there are any coincidences or that things just happen by chance. Everything that happens in our lives is part of life's design. Life is so intricately designed that everyone who shares in our experience, from the time we are born till the time that we die, is a part of our life's design. I'll share with you my understanding of life design, and, most important, I will help you to explore *your* relationship to the system of life's design.

While life's design is helpful in understanding how and why things happen in our everyday existence, that perspective is only a small part of what life is about. Ultimately, this book is about helping you to understand the events and circumstances of your life and their relation to the bigger picture of life itself.

Over the years I've had various people give me advice on life, and collectively what they came up with is: 'God is testing you, so he sent you life lessons to see how devoted you are to him, and in the process he is making you stronger.'

Can you imagine pouring out your heart and soul to people and all they can come up with is the old conventional "wisdom," which is that God is testing you to make you stronger? This so-called "explanation" wasn't enough for me to make sense of what was happening in my life. I noticed that this theory of God and his relationship to life experiences as a way of testing one's faith was a common underlying theme shared by many of my friends and family. But a lot of these bare-boned concepts about God and life just weren't feeding my spirit.

I consider myself to be a highly spiritual person, spiritual in the sense that I know what thoughts, words, and deeds work best for my spirit. I know when I am comfortable experiencing peace within my soul by the ways in which I choose to live my life. I choose to be in harmony with my vibrations. I choose to have control over my emotional state by applying my own philosophical practices.

Over time I began to theorize and formulate the rules by which I wanted to govern my life. It was clear that I wanted to be a good person, and to be a good person I know that I have to do, think, and say good things. I know that to be good I must be kind and loving and honest. It followed that to be a bad person meant doing the opposite of what it means to be good. I would have to be unkind, unloving, and dishonest to consider myself a bad person. Going into my preteen years, I began to look at the world in this simple way, resolving to use *my own* understanding of life and my relation to it from then on.

With my early adult years came disappointment over relationships. I sought the counsel of friends and family members. Their well-meaning advice, intended to assuage my emotional woes, was again that <u>God is testing you to make you a better and stronger person</u>. But no matter which way I looked at the notion of a God who was testing me, my spirit wasn't connecting with that message—not at all! It was not in vibrational alignment with the ways I'd been practicing control over my emotional and ethereal life. My practice involves surrendering to life and controlling my ego rather than having ego control me. But for the most part, I took their advice for what it was, but it wasn't enough for me. So I sought to understand my inner turmoil by reading and listening to various self-help, inspirational, spiritual, and personal growth books and CDs. Some of the concepts and inspirations in these books resonated with me and spoke to my life personally.

I took a particular liking to Hay House Publishing, noting that many of my favorite books came from Hay House's stable of authors. I am sure it has published books from a great many authors, but for the most part no matter which book or audio book I chose from this publisher, the messages seemed one and the same. I could, of course, distinguish one author from the next by looking at the title and reading the dust jacket, but for the most part their messages were strikingly similar. So I see Hay House as a genre of its own, with each of its authors spinning essentially the same conclusions in their own individual ways.

Still, I will continue to purchase books from Hay House, and for pretty much the same reason one views a favorite movie over and over again—you never get sick and tired of it.

Ultimately, though, nothing I was listening to and none of the advice I was receiving was satisfying my core. Not until I decided to put pen to paper and make sense of my life did things begin to fall into place and metamorphose into pages and pages of what I thought and how I lived my life. This is how my book came into being.

I've written in the straightforward and informal way I would like to be spoken to. My hope is that the next time you seek advice about how to live a life that is happy and good, you'll consider what you've read here, rather than a statement as desperately evasive as 'God is testing you to make you stronger.'

I've long known that I have a natural talent for thinking about life and its relation to me. I know too that the people closest to me would agree that I've always had a gift for understanding life and the ways that we live it.

Over the years, I've had very close friendships with people who were my senior by 10, 20, 30, and even 40 years. I would not only be their very good friend, but an advisor to them as well. And while we would use each other interchangeably for advice, I would speak from my heart and they would speak to me based on experience. I knew there was something a little different about me when my mother's girlfriends would become my long-term close friends.

I had previously believed that I am an old soul—that is, that the soul that animates my body is that of an older, much wiser person. I've come to regard that old-soul theory as untrue in my assessment of my life. While having an old soul generally tends to be regarded as an indication of being wise beyond one's years, the expression "old soul" does not necessarily mean that one literally has an old soul. Life gives us the devices needed to succeed in our worldly missions. If that means one must be wise beyond their years, so it shall be in the unfolding of one's life. It is the same in any other way that we are gifted by life—a special skill, a beautiful singing voice, a gift for comedy—whatever is needed to carry out our destinies is ours. So much of what we think of as luck is actually a part of our creation from before we were born. I believe that in the creation of my existence my purpose in life was to contribute to the literature of the here and now. The clarity that I experience is none other than a means that life has given to me to carry out my life's mission. It isn't that clarity was granted to me instantly; exposure to the material world awakened that knowledge that was always a part of my being. My understanding of the world is concurrent with the here and now and not the carry-over of an older, much wiser soul. It is Spirit and Source, streaming consciousness in the now.

When I look at the progression of my life, I can see that I was destined to become a writer. My closet is full of composition notebooks containing stories that I wrote as a child. I have won numerous story competitions throughout middle school and high school for my ideas on life and how the mind works even before I looked into theories and philosophies. In the seventh grade I wrote a story based on the main character having schizophrenia before I understood what schizophrenia meant. It wasn't until my mother proofread my story that she told me my protagonist had schizophrenia, a physiological disorder. Needless to say, that was one of the competitions that I won.

The reason I'm telling you a little bit about my background is to speak to my point of understanding our purpose in this world. This book is written to speak to you about some of the things I've come to understand and live by as truth in the discovery of the self. I will give further details of my life story in the introduction to illustrate my point of how I've come to understand life and our relationship to life as a people in the grand scheme of things.

This book is not simply about my life or about me. It is about giving you the confidence to help you make sense of your life in the midst of uncertainty and the morass of futile advice that we tend to get from our friends and family. While "God is testing you" is the standard advice you would get in the throes of disconnect from yourself, I am here to say that God has nothing to do with this disconnect.

In my understanding of God, he is the missing connection that makes you and me whole. He is supposed to be there for you all the time to give you the comfort that you need. He is the Almighty King of Kings, and you need not worry about anything because he's got your back! So why would God like to test me? Why would God want to play games with me?

This book is not about God, or whether God is trying to test you or not. I am not here to argue the existence or nonexistence of God. I am not dismissing the theory that God is trying to test you via your adversities. Rather, I am saying that in the midst of uncertainty, God doesn't have to be your cover for the unknown; just accept that time and patience will give you all that you seek to find.

Whether I believe in God or not is not what this book is about. I will speak of my affiliation to religion and God in my introduction. My relationship and understanding of God should not impact the message of this book, nor should it impact your mission in understanding yourself. But I do have to mention God because God was the advice that I got from my family and friends when I had to deal with the woes of my life experiences. The idea of God is very much alive in our existence, whether we accept it or not.

This book is about being honest. If I cannot be honest with you about life, how can I help you understand your role in this lifetime? While God is not the central focus of this book, it is a concept that we encounter often. Allow me to inspire you. If all you get out of this book is a little bit of inspiration to welcome change into your life, I will have done my job. Allow me to give you my heart in exchange for a little bit of your heart. I love you and want to see you get ahold of yourself and know that the disconnect you are experiencing is only temporary. The best thing about life is that it's ever-changing, so you may feel one way today and, thankfully, a different way tomorrow.

While this is a self-help book, I am not here to sugarcoat reality. I will speak about the things that will be relevant to your journey in the 21st century. At times, my examples may seem shocking, but they are necessary to convey the points that I am making.

I hope that you take away a new way of living and a new perspective on your life. I hope your journey becomes more fulfilling and rewarding after reading this book. I hope you will develop a new and useful attitude about how you wish to live your life from now on.

Love,
Karissa

Acknowledgments

There are so many wonderful people in my life! I am just thankful that I can call them friends; Dr. Richard Saland, Linda Evans, Sabrina Miller, Sandra Davis, and Eleanor Delibero, I thank you! To my editor Jo-Ann Langseth,—thank you; you've made my dream come true! Finally, to my best and closest friend of all time my mother, Kathleen Thomas. I thank you, Mom, for being the person that you are. You are truly someone to look up to and you constantly inspire me. I love you for that.

Introduction

Can someone help me understand this life? Is there any reason as to why I am here? Why can't I make sense of things? How can it be that everything that happens in my life is for the highest good? Why am I so confused, and why are things taking so long to happen? These are some of the questions that most people ask themselves daily about life and about their individual existence. You are not alone in asking these questions; in fact, we all ask these questions throughout our lives. It doesn't matter how old you are or how things are going in your life; from time to time we just ask ourselves these very intimate and fundamental questions about our existence. Whether or not you are upfront about your doubts regarding your raison d'etre, we all struggle to understand why we are here. Those of us who don't dwell too much on these questions just accept their existence for what it appears to be. But, from time to time, we silently (or loudly) ask, why am I here? And/or why do I have to leave?

Life is designed so that you can fulfill what you have come into form to experience. And, life acts so that everything works in your favor surrounding your reason for living. In most cases, it isn't until looking back on your journey that you appreciate the circumstances surrounding your life. It may seem as though everything that has happened just fell right into place for you; you may be tempted to call this perfect timing, an ongoing synchronicity, or simply the mystery of life. In any case, I'm sure you've heard the saying that life has its own way of mysteriously working things out, and in your favor. I think life is not a willy-nilly phenomenon; I think life is intelligently designed.

My belief is that we co-created our emergence into being, and that life just sets things in place to help us achieve our worldly mission. We inspire life to bring us into form. After all, it is our divine right and privilege to express our divinity. And this divine right is just part of how life was designed. For example, you don't question why a car has a fancy design; that's just the way it is made. All you know is that you like that design so you buy the car.

You cannot allow yourself to get caught up in the detailing of life and its design. Just know that life, like the things that we know and accept into being, works the same way—it is just a part of its design.

Divinity underlies life's design. Purpose is also essential to life's design, as is wisdom. Perhaps the fundamental question about life is: Who's designing it? We can easily identify the design ("make") of a car that we like—we know that it's a Mr. Honda, Mr. Lexus, or Ms. Mercedes-Benz design, but whose design is *life's*? We don't question the design of the cars that we like much beyond naming them. We just accept that they are what they are and that somebody at some point designed those cars. I am sure there is a specialized marketing team that comes up with new models of the cars we like, but we don't really care who's involved in the process. All we know is that it's a brand we are attracted to, and that's all there is to it.

So who's the chief architect of life's design? God, I suppose! Or maybe the human concept of God is just one of the mysticisms of life's design. Life has been life for so long—some say it has always been—that we can't trace it back to the day it began or how it started. All we can do is accept that life is, and that it works. Life works so well, in fact, that part of its design is that we fulfill our destiny, the destiny that we co-created with life. In looking at life in a co-created way gives you ownership in your existence. An accepted existence in return gives you a sense of control over your life. An accepted sense of self in turn results in appreciation of the self; in the gratification of your existence and the acceptance of your life the universe responds in favor of your being. I don't think that this co-creation is such a radical or far-fetched idea, because it has worked in that mysterious co-creating way for me.

As a child, I watched my grandmother practice Hinduism. Representations of the Hindu gods and goddesses hung in the center of my living room. But, while Hinduism was the centerpiece around which my grandmother raised her children, her children chose other religious paths. I attended Catholic Mass with my aunt some Sundays, and I saw my mother attending a Baptist church. I also attended a Pentecostal church with my best friend who lived next door. Being a part of these different expressions of faith enabled me to accept and understand the various points of view of each faith.

It wasn't until hearing from the Pentecostal church I was attending that if I practiced any other faith, I would be doomed to hell and barred from heaven, that I began to entertain serious questions.

I didn't welcome the narrow-minded notion that if you failed to serve the one-and-only God enthroned in heaven, you wouldn't make it through the Pearly Gates. After all, I grew up in a Hindu home where I saw various gods as important to my well-being. Mind you, at this point I was eight years old and learning in school that dinosaurs roamed the Earth. I was also learning through this Christian faith that dinosaurs did not roam the Earth and that there were no such things as dinosaurs.

What I was learning in school and what I was learning at church just wasn't adding up for me. So I abandoned that church because all it told me was that my entire way of life had doomed me to everlasting hellfire. Alliance with various faiths and my belief in dinosaurs would be more than enough damning evidence for St. Peter!

To me, it didn't matter at all what faith you practiced, as I respected the various beliefs and practices of my grandmother, mother, best friend, and aunt. Just knowing we are part of something as unfathomable as life is so mind-boggling that people don't know what to make of it. I think I had to take part in Roman Catholicism, Hinduism, Buddhism, and the Baptist faith to fulfill my purpose. I had to be exposed to several major religions to end up in no religion at all. I had to part ways with religion in order to find spirituality within myself.

Over the years this spiritual awareness took on a life of its own, manifesting in ways that I now know were preparing me for this very moment; this moment of clarity. For now I can elaborate with certainty my purpose and mission in this life. As spirit moved within and connected with my co-created, divine quest in life, I am now able to make sense of all that has happened along my journey.

Looking back on the projects I worked on pre-college and during college, I can see that all of them revolved around understanding that relationship with spirit and with Source. Of course at the time, I just thought I was being creative; I had no idea that spirit, as part of the intricate design of life, was unfolding my quest before my very eyes. In 1998, I was taking a psychology course at the Borough of Manhattan Community College in New York as part of a bridge-to-college program. I was so influenced by the course that I later wrote a story. This story developed into a script that I wrote for a contest that Showtime, the premium cable channel, was sponsoring.

I was then attending a bridge-to-college program at New York University, where I was taking a music class on Johann Sebastian Bach. In this class two very important things happened: I fell in love with classical music and I started dating a young man who was a film student at Tisch School of the Arts at NYU.

Life is so attuned to guiding us on our spiritual quests! Almost immediately, I learned that classical is the music that I will listen to throughout my life to help me connect and harmonize with my divine self. It is through classical music that I am able to channel my well-being back into a safe place with spirit when I need to be in direct connection with Source.

The young man I dated enabled me to see that through film, I would be able to visualize my connection to Source. But of course at the time, I had no clue that video was going to be a prominent means that I would use to make sense of this eager spirit within.

So when Showtime had the video contest, it was a perfect opportunity for Source to express directly through me. I now had a script and had been awakened by this young man who'd shown me that video is an apparatus perfect for what is to follow in my life. My script, "The Fear of the Subconscious," was submitted to Showtime, and was among their top 100 choices. My script made the next cut of the top 25 applicants and then it was out. I was crushed. It was the summer of 1998. School was out, and I was devastated.

At this time video wasn't a major part of any high school curriculum, and in fact, DVDs and mini DVDs weren't even in existence. The Internet was not commonly used around this time, piquing everyone's curiosity. My high school, The Institute for Collaborative Education, purchased a VHS camcorder to jump on the bandwagon of technological innovation. After learning I hadn't made the next round of selections for the Showtime video contest, I went straight to my Assistant Principal, Brett Schneider, and told him what happened with the contest. I asked him to lend me the school camcorder because I was going to make the video anyway. He supported the notion and purchased a more updated editing program called Strata, downloaded it onto his computer at work, and gave me access to his office the entire summer of 1998 to work on my video project.

Life is so meticulously designed for each individual that things happen the way they should, regardless of any obstacles that you may think are in your way. I was compelled to make that video to create a visual representation of what my spirit was trying to tell me. I was not yet crystal clear as to exactly what that was. When school reconvened in the fall I was now in my senior year of high school. I joined New York City's ACT-SO, a program that promotes academic and artistic excellence among African-American students. I submitted my video, "The Fear of the Subconscious," in the final competition of this program, was awarded a gold medal, and headed for the National Competition in New Orleans. I didn't win a gold medal nationally, but one of the panel judges sought me out on judgment day to personally tell me that my video was amazing. He explained that while it was gold-medal qualified, the judging panel had chosen an animation. At that time animation and video were both in the same category. He said regardless of the judges' choice that I should not give up because he believed I would go far in my life. He said I had so much potential that I should trust and believe that all will work out for me.

I was crushed. Here comes this man telling me my video was "golden," but that it wasn't going to win, and don't take it personally! When I got back to New York, I submitted that video to The Jay Sanders Film Festival, and was awarded Honorary Mention. In my senior year of high school I also participated in the Sophie Davis Bridge to Medicine Program. I thought I wanted to be a doctor. This program was a crucial factor in what was to ultimately lead me to understanding the purpose that would fulfill my destiny. I studied and stayed in this program for an entire year. My grades were average to below average. I got B's and C's (and even F's on my chemistry tests). I just wasn't connecting to these classes. The program director, Ms. Jerome, sat me down in her office and asked me if I was really serious about becoming a doctor because my grades weren't showing that I could handle the course work. Of course, I resented her comments and completed the program. In telling me I wasn't capable of becoming a doctor, she was certainly challenging my ego! But it wasn't really that I was incapable; rather, I wasn't listening to Source telling me that I had not come into existence for that experience.

This experience, however, served to show me that my path in life wasn't supposed to be that of a doctor, and although I love science and I am very curious about biology, that wasn't the deal I signed up for when I co-created my existence here on Earth.

I went to college and studied new media, with a concentration in film. Stubborn as I was, I minored in biology, taking all my pre-med classes just in case I changed my mind and wanted to go to medical school. But, just as in the earlier program, I couldn't get better grades than B's and C's in chemistry. My spirit kept right on trying to tell me, in the most obvious way possible, that becoming a doctor wasn't what I came here to do.

Meanwhile, my video projects spoke to my deepest beliefs, and I kept cranking out work having to do with spirit and my connection to spirit. Of course, all these projects happened divinely and without me even comprehending what I was actually doing. Again, I just thought I was being creative. Some of the videos I've created are: *Subliminal Chance, The Quest to Happiness,* and *Le Fantôme* (the ghost, in French). My senior project expressed my philosophies and my understanding of life.

So the theme that wended through my college days explored this very deep desire that I shared with my spirit about life and understanding it. Again, this happened unconsciously and was simply a natural part of my well-being.

After college and over the next eight years I learned firsthand through life experiences, especially the trials and tribulations of being in a committed relationship, getting married, and working through a failing relationship that I had some learning to do. And it was in the rediscovery of myself that I was able to find the words to write this book. It was through the reconnection to self that I could retrieve and build upon many of the thoughts I'd had about life and its meaning. It was through the process that I will describe in this book that I was able to get back on track and reconnect with spirit and ultimately with Source.

I've shared these stories from my life mainly to make the point that everything is relevant in the grand scheme of things. I am sure you've discovered this to be also true for yourself as you reflect on your life and on the journey you've taken. Looking back on my life, I understand and deeply appreciate that everything turned out the way it was supposed to. Everything that has happened up to this point in my life has conspired to put me right here in this moment, writing this book for you.

It wasn't until my mother suggested one day that I read John 3:16 that all the pieces came together. The King James Version of John 3:16 states: "*For God so loved the world that he gave his only begotten Son, that whosoever believeth in him should not perish, but have everlasting life.*" It was in that moment that life spoke to me, that it all started to make sense to me. Although John 3:16 is the most popular Bible scripture for Christians, and millions can relate to it, to me it speaks of an explicit understanding of what I have come here to do. I've come to give people a better understanding of living so that they may enjoy eternal life here on Earth! My 3/16 birthday served as the direct means that Source has used to lead me right to this Bible verse.

I have long been aware that a humanitarian lives within me. The will to share and help others is an integral part of who I am.

While this journey is still unfolding, with "miles to go before I sleep," I continue to embrace this understanding, ever open to the inflow of wisdom.

It is in constant recognition of the spirit within and the circumstances without that I am able to fulfill my life purpose to write and share my philosophies about life and humanity.

There is definitely a movement afoot in the 21st century, and that movement involves the reconnection to self and to purpose. I know I was born to be in this movement, that I wanted to be here right now in this generation to experience this flowering in self-development.

1

Life Unfolding

Uncertainty, understanding, patience, time, value, love, hope, peace, and purpose are just some of the words that resonate within, when we start thinking and talking about our lives. To truly understand what we are doing here takes self-awareness, belief, and trust. Life is a state and a system in which spirit has come to be present in form. Life is spirit. Spirit is life unfolding. Spirit is everything that life is, connecting you forever to Source as long as spirit lives within. Accept it or not, but you've come into existence not by the choice of your parents but by the will for existence that you co-created with Source to be here, in the here and now.

Accept that you are part of life, and spirit will unfold in the ways it ought to for you. Believe that you are part of the most profound and elaborate system of design, the design of life. Understand that life is designed in your best interest. It is a hard concept to accept that life is catering to you all the time, but it is true, even if the outcome isn't always as you predict. Even if you're having a difficult time in this moment and things just aren't happening the way you want them to, you must trust that life will not disappoint you. Life is so much in favor of our growth and happiness that cries are only to be followed by smiles. Patience is only to be followed by peace. Pain is only to be followed by joy.

Life unfolding is a beautiful thing, and while it may seem that life is unpredictable and scary, it is just unawareness of your consciousness that has led you to this dreary scary place within. It may seem that life can take you places you never prepared yourself for, but in actuality everything is as it should be; it is all part of the alignment and perfect attunement of your individual existence to life. Spirit guides this life, so embrace all that is.

Embrace all that is when life presents itself to you. Life sometimes forces you to learn both toughness and forgiveness so that it can give you wisdom. Knowledge gained from your experiences is indispensable. Once understanding is acquired, it cannot be taken away by anyone. The awareness that now informs your being prepares you for continuing life lessons, and with each new experience, your understanding expands a little bit more.

The Lessons

Life lessons are for you and for you alone. It's difficult to tell someone how to live their life or to even explain to them the correct steps in overcoming some of the many hurdles that one must bear. No matter how much you protest and preach, people must dabble in their own life experience. While you may be inclined to walk alongside your children to show them, step by step, what you have found to be pitfalls and stumbling blocks, they too must learn to fall so that they too can learn how to get up. It is in the getting up from our falls that we learn the most about life. These lessons prepare us for the next round of what is to come in our life experience.

It is in the upward impetus that comes from being down that we experience life's lessons. Sometimes when you are down it is hard to get up. But it is in those moments of getting up that you find the beauty and wisdom in your relationship to others.

Sometimes you truly need to let go of certain people and allow others to help you stand when you are down. Sometimes it is in crying and hurting that you begin to gain strength for future hurts and pains. And it is in this strength that you discover your courage. It is in this strength that you find your true voice. It is in this strength that you take ownership of your existence.

Falling and getting up are necessary parts of life unfolding. We have all experienced falling down and bruising our bodies. Sometimes after a fall a scar remains and, over time, that scar heals. A healing physical wound can be seen in the same light as the healing that can follow an emotional fall. Emotional falls do leave scars, often causing us to avoid that particular pitfall for the rest of our life because we are afraid to get hurt again. But no matter how much we try to run from emotional pain, we inevitably experience it, and it is through suffering and the loss of loved ones that we learn some of our most uplifting lessons.

Death is as much a part of living as living is a part of dying. Every day we get older, and every day we are preparing to leave this body. Death is inevitable, and all must face it head-on.

The journey of life can consume and overwhelm us; we can find ourselves lost and bewildered at times. But if you keep learning and growing, you can certainly find your way to fulfillment. Sometimes we get stuck in these challenges and find ourselves asking, "Why me?" We cannot see beyond the question. For any growth to happen, we must get beyond that why, changing the question to: *How can I get beyond this point in my life?* How can I find the strength I need to pass through and leave behind my own mental anguish? Stopping and reflecting is sometimes the only way to get beyond a "why me?" stalemate.

While you are essentially independent of others, people are yet a part of life's design to work in support of your existence. The people I'm referring to are ageless, colorless, and classless; any person embodying a spirit from Source can impact our life. People are people, carrying out their own destinies, just as we are. They look the same as we do and feel the same as we do. We are all together in this life to communicate and, whenever possible, to love one another. People can serve as helpful guides in our lives. They can be our teachers to help us grow in a positive way and to aid us in our life's journey. People can also act as distractions who try to hinder us from advancing to where we ought to be. Yet even from them we gain wisdom, and ultimately find our way to where we need to be.

The Signs

Resistance from people can push us forward into a better understanding of ourselves. Resistance, too, is a part of life's design, working independently of our consciousness and in complete connection with Source to get us into an experience that can bring about wisdom. Resistance in personal relationships at first glance appears to be a negative. For example: For whatever reason, a person's spirit doesn't accept you. It may seem strange because you've done nothing to this person. But for whatever reason, they just don't like you. As an emotional being, you will usually feel disturbed and offended when someone doesn't like you. However, that resistance prevents a relationship from developing between you and that person. You are better off allowing that resistance to simply be, as the disconnect is actually a positive thing. It tells you that a relationship between you and the other person will not be in alignment with Source, and that the disconnect will forever be present in that relationship. When you feel this resistance, honor it by letting the relationship go.

You cannot force a connection between yourself and another person if the connection does not exist. While you may feel strongly toward the person and you may actually value his or her opinion of you, you cannot expect the connection to be stronger than what it is. Not everybody who comes into our lives is meant to be a part of it forever. People come and go. You cannot let the traffic of people coming and going cause gridlock, keeping you from moving forward with your life mission.

I personally know about being stuck and not moving forward. I know how it feels to find myself doing things out of character just to get an answer to "why me?" Had I been aware enough to ask how I could get beyond the situation, I probably would not have spent so much time wallowing in self-pity. While most of us do, at one time or another, carry a "why me" burden on our backs, I urge you to get beyond that and move on to the learning part of your experience.

Confronting Ourselves

One of the hardest things to do is to confront ourselves about ourselves. We are so critical of our mistakes and so distraught about our stumbling blocks that it can be hard to take an honest look at ourselves. But often we forget that we are not acting of our own accord; we all have spirit within us, and sometimes we become so disconnected from that spirit that our ego erupts in self-criticism. Rather than telling you to go easy on yourself, I would suggest that you pay much closer attention to all that is within the self, becoming more aware of your choices and decisions so you can avoid hurting yourself.

Life-course choices and decisions are some of the harder ones to make because the results aren't immediately clear. Be smart about the choices that you make. Before choosing any course of action, ask yourself these five questions:

1. Can I live with myself if I made that choice?
2. What are some of the possible consequences of my decision?
3. Is this something I could live with and not regret for the rest of my life?

4. Is this choice in harmony with my vibrational alignment?
5. Is this where I need to be in my life right now?

After you've determined that the decisions you've made are in alignment with your life mission, go ahead and declare immediate action! At this point, a declaration of your intent is put into place in the universe. Make sure your answers to the questions you're asking flow in a realm of positives so you can stream well-being into your experience. For instance: You've decided to get in shape and lose weight because you want a healthier life. You've agreed that you can live with the decision to want to live healthier. You've decided that the only thing that can result from a healthier lifestyle is better health and a longer lifespan. You've decided that this is a decision you're willing to commit to for the rest of your life and feel happy about. You've decided that the time has come to make this change, and it's where you need to be in your life. So you embrace this new approach to life and your health in a loving and warm way. You know that the outcome is something that will make you feel better, inside and out. You've begun to cultivate a positive attitude toward this change that you so desperately need in your life. Had you decided to lose weight and get in shape without a clear direction that would encourage a positive overall feeling, your weight-loss objectives would not be met, nor would you feel complete and fulfilled.

You're ready for the flow

Assuming that you've declared some changes and fostered positivism in your outlook, the next step is to embrace that flow of positive energy. Welcome the transformation and don't assign limits and specific expectations, but do encourage and welcome what you are experiencing. If by any chance you want to manifest a different outcome, then ask the five questions again, declare immediate transformation, and continue to embrace and engage in that experience.

You've been blessed with this one-time journey, and you should look at it with gratitude as the ultimate blessing! Your existence here on Earth is to serve as a beneficent presence here. You are to learn to embody love, wisdom, freedom, and the other major attributes. While later on in this book you'll discover why you are so special, I just want to say now that you shouldn't take yourself or your existence for granted. Seek the simple treasures that fulfill you. We all have within ourselves these "simple gifts" of self-fulfillment, which may be experienced in laughing, smiling, and, above all, a full connection to Source.

When I talk about Source, I am not referring to a far-fetched abstract concept. I am talking about an energy that is far bigger than we are, and omnipresent within us and outside of us. Source is the force that governs us, the One Power so great that sometimes we just want to spontaneously shout and give praise and thanks. This force may be called God, Source, Creator, the One, and any number of names. Obviously, it is not a bearded gent who sits in heaven, but energy so loving and powerful that all we really want to do is bask in that light and get to know it. It is in searching for God that we discover more of ourselves, because God lives within each and every one of us. It is undeniable that this force of energy ignites within us all inspiration. Whenever we do or see something we love, that indescribable joy that we feel, that natural high that courses through us is what I am talking about. That force can be none other than Source, residing within us and speaking to us in the language of joy.

The flow of joy

Joy is so much a part of us! In our natural state of well-being, we can effortlessly access it all the time. Sometimes we lose sight of where we are in life and forget that joy is in our heart and our soul. Joy is built into our being and constitutes our well-being. Joy is a very personal thing. I suggest that you write a list to remind yourself of what brings you joy so that when you are down and out, you can remember and find the joy that lives within your soul. A list may look something like this: Putting glue on my hand and then peeling it off; drawing a rainbow with crayons of all different colors; and sitting in front of a fireplace absorbing the energy of the fire. Joy is such a personal thing, but it is also a simple thing. Learn to access your inner joy and let it shine for all to see and adore.

So much of this journey is for you to become more of yourself, and for you to be who you are destined to be. So much of what you do is to get you closer to where you need to be in spirit. While the journey may become confusing and cluttered with people and things, I encourage you to detach yourself from these people and things from time to time and "re-set" and refocus on your spirit. Sometimes the only way to know that you've gone someplace is for you to look back and see the road you've traveled. But don't wait to always look behind yourself to see where you've been. Let the journey be a conscious and deliberate effort. Continue to look forward and embrace your journey as a pleasant and rewarding experience for as long as you're fortunate to be on this planet.

The flow of balance

So much of life involves careful preparation and planning. Have a clear roadmap you want to follow, so you can use it to guide you. This roadmap lies within your imagination, so see yourself "going places" within your mind. If that place is to end up being a doctor, for example, know that you must be tremendously disciplined and seek mentorship in your pursuit of financing and the appropriate pre-med classes and medical school. From time to time stop and reflect; never get caught up in one aspect of your life's journey. In other words, don't just focus on career and neglect every other aspect of what it means to live. You have to create balance. You often have to multitask while you are here on Earth. Find out the steps that will take you to the career you desire, and embark at your earliest opportunity! But also consider those who are close to you and show them ongoing love and appreciation.

Balance all aspects of your journey and it will be much more rewarding and fulfilling to your soul. See yourself as a cross-country freight train, and every car that you pull as being equally important. Each one carries something different, and so you end up hauling hundreds of boxcars, but it is, of course, imperative that when the train arrives at its final destination, all the cars arrive together.

Take time to focus on one aspect at a time, but at the same time seek out the other parts to the puzzle. Say you are putting together a 10,000-piece puzzle and you have the picture in front of you of an underwater scene. Initially, you spend all your time finding the pieces to the shark and behold! You do find all the shark pieces, but the rest of the puzzle is still missing and incomplete! Here you've spent all your time picking out the pieces to the shark, and all you have to show for it is imbalance. You haven't attended to the entire plan. Remember that time is usually in a big hurry, and you just might not have enough of it to complete your puzzle! So balance is very important in trying to figure out this thing called life.

The flow of Consciousness

Fortunately, we have consciousness to guide our decision-making process. Our human consciousness informs this process, but it can turn a blind eye to spirit and Source; as a result, ego can, and very often does, overtake consciousness and dominate your logic. Ego is a superficial and fundamentally false view of self. In most cases it acts to mask insecurity, or a fear of being unaware. Ego is not permanent by any means, and sometimes people need to, in a sense, remain in ignorance in order to become knowledgeable. A new profound understanding of self that derives from overcoming ego is liberating.

People are so afraid of the unknown that when they pretend to be something other than what they are, they overwhelm themselves with a false sense of self. Everything that happens in life doesn't have to be known and in fact *cannot be known,* so stop trying to figure it all out! Let the unknown be unknown to you. Trust in spirit and in Source that all essentials will be available to you in the right way and at the right time. If you have a plan, stick to it and spirit will lead you to where you need to be. Spirit will always guide you, delivering you to where you need to be and amongst the right people every time.

The flow of love/spirit

If you listen to your heart and follow your smiles, they will always lead you down the right path. Feeling really good about something is the indication that you're on track; feeling not so good is the sign to knowing when you're veering off track. Keep making the right choices for yourself and take a stand against being naïve. If you listen wholeheartedly to your inner self and you trust in the design of life, you will always be on track in your life. You must believe in yourself! You must know that you've come into the world to be more than what you appear to be; you are here for a purpose that you co-created with Source.

You must accept that you are here to primarily develop yourself and yourself alone. You are independent of others and you should not cling to them, for they have come into being just as you have, to fulfill a destiny. Know that you are on a mission to discover that passion within yourself. If you're not sure what your passion is, don't stress over it; it will come to you when you least expect it. Your passion is a part of you. It is built in to you, and your spirit knows and will guide you to it. Your passion is tied into your purpose, so don't overlook or undervalue what you are passionate about.

My mother is very passionate about music and the piano. She made it to grade six in music and stopped at age 18. However, music is so much a part of her passion that at age 49, she decided to get back into it and complete all levels necessary to become a master musician. By practicing and getting a piano teacher to help her to honor her passion, she is now able the think bigger about what she wants to do with her talent and is putting in place the steps necessary to start her own charter school specializing in music. Although my mother is very accomplished and has two master's degrees in education, music was always her first love. Having to take music tests with teenagers and other youths hasn't bothered her in the least because, as she nears age 50, she is pursuing her passion. She is truly ecstatic about "following her bliss," amazed with herself and elated about her progress.

Get excited, knowing that you are on a mission. Get excited about yourself. It is healthy to get excited about the things that motivate you. Positive, joyous feelings bloom within your soul when you get excited by your inspirations. Feeling good is how you know you're on track to where you need to be in the here and now.

2

Life Experiences

A life experience is everything that we encounter and that we give meaning to. Life is an experience from the moment we enter the world until the time we leave. Being able to identify and create relationships with things and people is a fundamental aspect of our existence. It is through our own understanding that life becomes an experience. Events and circumstances happen in our lives that enable us to gain deeper understanding and acceptance of ourselves. As an integral part of life's design, life experiences work ceaselessly for self-betterment. Life experiences teach us lessons and in turn, those lessons are expressed as experiences.

It is important to pay close attention to the feelings that arise when you're confronted with events or circumstances. Feelings are your direct connection to Source, communicating to you about that circumstance. It is in feeling good that you know that that situation is happening in perfect alignment, and it is in a bad feeling about the situation that Source is telling you that you cannot get so comfortable with that circumstance or situation, because in the long run that's not where you're supposed to be. It is in accepting the feelings that you are experiencing, and accepting the situation and/or circumstance to mean what it is supposed to mean—whether good or bad—that enables you to grow. We can, therefore, welcome all experience.

Once you accept a situation or circumstance for what it is supposed to offer, you are in good shape, because now you are able to wisely determine your next move. Your next move is usually to continue with that experience, or to let it go. As human beings we are an emotional and inquisitive species, what we generally tend to do is hold on to an experience that we must release.

Letting go isn't easy, nor is it fun. Letting go will be painful. Memories will always leave an indelible imprint on your psyche as long as you are alive and in good health. Sometimes you may even want to cry, because when you reflect on the pain that you've endured, it returns full-force, and can feel overwhelming. Consciousness resurrects all the little details that you somehow overlooked while that experience was taking place.

Your consciousness informs you that you were always present in the moments of that experience, but chose to ignore your ill-willed feelings and misgivings. You ignored your connection to Source, telling you that this is a feel-bad situation and that you need to let go of this experience a.s.a.p.! Consciousness is always with you, and consciousness will always replay details from your life. Therefore, you will probably never fully forget all the times you've cried and experienced emotional distress. There's no doubt that letting go of an event or person in your life is going to be hard at first, but over time, you will begin to genuinely smile again.

Resentment

One result of letting go of situations or of people in your life may be bitterness. Resentment about your past is yet another hurdle you will have to overcome if you cannot move on without animosity. Anger will be a stumbling block you will surely face in the process of letting go. However, the secret is to be brutally honest with where you are with yourself. Admit that you aren't perfect and that your every contribution to the situation was not golden. Admit that you are an emotional being caught up in an unloving or unproductive situation, and that you fueled the situation and allowed it to get the best of you. Take back ownership of your life and move beyond the anger. Put out the fires of rage in your soul with the cooling waters of forgiveness. Forgive those who have brought you grief, and forgive yourself for your own role in the situation, even if it was mainly oblivion.

Healthy vs. Unhealthy Relationship

Relationships are the woof and the weave of life's design. They are of course necessary for procreation as well as communication. We look alike, we desire alike, and we need each other to fulfill our destinies. We play off each other to learn and grow as individuals. But there are healthy and unhealthy relationships, and it is imperative that we learn to recognize the difference. I know the difference because I was able to live the difference! And by telling you the difference, I can only hope that it will save you from enduring my lessons!

In a healthy relationship, you feel good about yourself. You feel good about life—you just feel good. Your self-worth is beyond question, and embraced. You feel equal. You feel that you are contributing as much as your partner. You feel valued and respected. You communicate in a loving and supportive way. You listen to each other and talk to each other.

In an unhealthy relationship, you feel bad most of the time. You feel discouraged and you feel that the relationship is out of balance. You feel as if you are giving more than you are receiving. Your self-worth is constantly under attack. You, in turn, feel small, inadequate, and unworthy. You are afraid and on guard most of the time. You are under constant criticism, whether subtly or overtly, about your physical appearance, your behavior, and/or your mental capabilities—either you're too smart or too dumb. While in an unhealthy relationship, you have to choose your words carefully because you're uncertain about the response you'll get from your mate. Your words must be tailored "just so," either to please or to avoid misunderstanding.

Recognizing the difference between a healthy versus an unhealthy relationship is critical to the future or demise of that relationship. A relationship takes "two to tango." You may be in a healthy space in your life while the person you're involved with is in a dysfunctional space—an unhealthy imbalance!

You have to know if the balance in the relationship makes you feel good. You have to know if a balance exists at all. You have to know if the relationship is equal as opposed to its feeling unequal.

Relationships teach us a great deal about ourselves. And when I speak of relationships, I am talking about all relationships that we develop, from friendships to marriages and everything in between. Relationships enable us to develop empathy, the ability to walk in another's shoes. They test our values and the commitment that we have to ourselves. Stick to your standards, and your relationships will no longer test your values and your self-commitments. Let your relationships open you like a blossoming flower, so that you may share from your core and shed sweetness all around. Let your relationship mirror what you stand for.

Marriage and You

In a marriage you can and in fact should maintain your identity, your own strong sense of self. We are all human beings here on this planet for our own development, and although we may "hook up" with somebody, that doesn't change the fact that we are here to experience our existence. A marriage may be seen as a lifetime bonus! A healthy, loving, selfless, union between two people is a beautiful thing. However, at least fifty percent of us marry under those circumstances and somehow things change and we end up in disharmony with our mates. Your life will be just as complete without a marriage as it would be with a marriage. Marriage isn't for everyone, and we shouldn't consume ourselves in chasing after that binding, contractual union. Binding relationship or not, people will do what they want to do. However, if you choose to marry someone, make sure that you are in total alignment and harmony with your mate so that the relationship isn't just another challenging responsibility. Make your marriage a *joy*—a union that fills you with gratitude as you explore and express the loving, selfless, and constantly growing fullness of yourself.

Friends and You

The requirements are the same for the friendships you build with people. The relationship should feel genuine. The relationship should feel balanced. The relationship should feel good, and it should feel natural. You should also feel good with your parents and children, and the harmony should be consistent in all your relationships. You should never feel "put upon"—that you are being overly compromising—and you shouldn't feel constantly under pressure. If you feel this way, ask your loved ones to back off and give you space, space in which to clear away the clutter in your mind, soul, and heart so that you may better embrace that relationship. You need to temporarily detach from everyone so that you can realign yourself with Source and, in turn, realign with others.

At the end of the day, we are all people. We are all people seeking to fulfill our own destinies. Allow and embrace that mission in all those whom you love. Allow people to be exactly who they truly are so that they can become more of who they want to be. This is what you wish for yourself, so apply the Golden

Rule and wish it for your loved ones as well. We are not always included in the plans of the people we love. More often than not, we are not to play a central role in what they need to experience, and for whatever reason the universe doesn't have us aligned with their experience. Embrace and accept the truth of where you stand relative to another.

Accepting the more difficult lessons of life will propel you to further experiences that are in alignment with you and your purposes. In order to learn what is, we must first pass over what is not. Every experience, rightly understood, will help you along your journey.

Adversity

Adversity is a necessary part of life experiences. The only thing you can do when faced with adversity is to experience it, learn from it, and move beyond it.

Can you really spare somebody from life's painful experiences? Can you prepare people for all the curves life is sure to throw their way? Can you help protect them from going through a particular challenge themselves? I would respond with a resounding NO to every one of these questions. Because people can be very stubborn, and sometimes life experiences itself is the only thing that can reassure a particular outcome. People have the tendency to be the believers of their own doing, but the wise ones save time by learning from others mistakes. Not under any circumstances can one prevent another from going through life experiences. For them to "take," the lessons learned need to be directly incorporated by the learner. Wisdom cannot be gained vicariously; it is a process that is gained, not acquired, over time. So does this mean that most young women will have to go through agonizing "love lessons" similar to my own to grow as an individual? As a mother, am I to sit by and watch my child, my daughter, go through grief just so that she can understand what love is, and is not? How can *any* loving mother protect her daughter from the lessons of life? Is there anything we can say or do to arm them against these "slings and arrows?" Can we protect the tender hearts of our daughters and sons? And I would say no, we can't. We just can't shield our children from their destined life lessons. You may persist: "But can't we at least prepare them in some way for what is likely to come?" And the reply to that question is simply no as well.

One way to look at life experiences is to recognize that they are all past tense. Life experiences are all relative to preexisting experiences that one has already lived. That's what makes them life EX-periences. And each one has taken us to the next level in life. Without each experience, there would have been no way for us to move forward in our lives. Life experiences are what build the strength, beauty, and individuality of each person.

So many of us struggle to comprehend our life experiences, and so many of us get lost in the process that we turn to our friends and family members for guidance. And still that void of uncertainty is not filled. Nothing can take the place of passing through an experience oneself to truly understand it. Ultimately, we discover that all the answers that we search for are within ourselves and within our understanding. This is why people often note that life is complicated. The complexity is born of the subjective and relative nature of all people and their experiences.

The deepest lesson life has to offer us individually lies in death, and especially our own death. In our absence from this world, from this planet Earth, from this particular and much loved body, life will still go on. Your neighbors will still rise every morning and brush their teeth. Chances are, you won't be on their minds. Imagine that! Even the people whom we cling to will live on after we are gone. Even those who attempt to "pass over" with someone else are still basically on their own, because they too, like everyone else, must return to Source. There may be no greater lesson than the lessons unlearned—no more a part of what life has to offer, not being around long enough to be honest with oneself. Often it is not until we are faced with the prospect of no longer being a "player" that we hustle to change our perspective on how we wish to live our lives. Never fail to live the way you want to! Don't succumb to the norm of societal standards! Don't capitulate to the vision of how your family and friends expect you to live your life. Be who you have come here to be! Don't wait for the Grim Reaper to come knocking before you truly live! Live *now* before death decides to snatch away this grandest of opportunities.

Self-Honesty

The first step begins with being honest with yourself about who you are and what you want to take from and give to this life. You must be able to confront your fears. You must learn from your experiences and clearly identify your conceptions and misconceptions about who you really are in this world. It is about coming clean with yourself. Self-honesty is about confessing and clearing up delusions and falsehoods that you harbor within yourself. For example: Lori wants to be perceived as a happy and successful woman, but she got pregnant out of wedlock. So she stays in a relationship that is not working so that people will admire her for being "a happily married wife and mother." But the truth is, she is an unloving wife, a neglectful mother, and an adulterer. It is clear that Lori is not being honest with herself about who she is and about what she wants from her life here on Earth. She may not have given it much thought, and may be acting on instinct alone.

This example is admittedly extreme, but it can possibly be the case, in various permutations, for thousands. Using this example, I will further discuss the ideal of self-honesty. Lori's circumstances stem from the fact that she is being dishonest with herself about who she is. It is her own misunderstanding and confusion about her values and morals that are causing the conflict.

Let's look at her situation again: Lori wants to be perceived as an admirable woman, but she got pregnant out of wedlock.

There are so many things wrong with this situation right from the git-go! And I could easily get sidetracked by focusing on education, gender roles, and a plethora of background issues. But the points are not that this woman got pregnant before marriage, is an unloving wife, a neglectful mother, and an adulteress. Those are only her symptoms. The cause of her many "illnesses" is that she does not "know herself," and is thus dishonest with herself. And when a person is dishonest with herself, that dishonestly feeds on itself, spiraling out of control and affecting everything and everyone in its path.

This woman endures an unpleasant journey for the sake of "appearances"—an image that she wants to portray to herself and mostly to others. This is an example of self-deception. Lori wants to do the right thing according to societal standards by marrying the father of her child. So she marries. And while her husband probably has something to do with why she behaves as she does, the major problem is that she is being dishonest with herself about what she wants out of life. Groping blindly in the dark, Lori is clearly unhappy. It is okay to admit that we are unhappy. The only way to deal with unhappiness is to acknowledge it and then find possible approaches to change your outlook and circumstances.

Aim to simplify your life. When you are dishonest about your motives and way of life, it always catches up with you. It affects your emotional and spiritual well-being. It brings confusion, chaos, and unhappiness to the lives of everyone involved. I'm going to break down the example above line by line and comment on the situation as I go along.

She wants to be perceived as an admirable woman. Stop worrying about how others perceive you. You are here, living, breathing, and doing the best you can.

She got pregnant out of wedlock. This is the 21st century and things are very different now. Most people are having sex before marriage. If you get pregnant when you are single—and that's a huge issue for you—abstain from having premarital sex from now on. If premarital sex conflicts with the morals and values that you have chosen to live by, honor the standards you've accepted and follow through on your word with a commitment that you make to yourself.

She stays in a relationship that is not working so that people will see her as successful. This is the time to be honest and accept that you are setting yourself up for unhappiness, because you already know your situation isn't working. See things the way they are, for there is nothing you can do about them unless you are first honest with yourself. Walking away now and moving on with your life, rather than bracing for additional psychological wear and tear, is the most loving thing you can do for yourself.

Who cares what people think? You are here for you, and while your situation is the way it is for now, honesty can definitely turn things around for you.

As a result she marries, but at home she is an unloving wife, a neglectful mother, and she commits adultery. Now this is a very extreme combination. What happens on the inside shows on the outside. Inner turmoil always results in outer mayhem. Lori's behavior suggests that there is a disconnect, and where there is a disconnect one cannot be happy.

Lori is clearly not contributing to life in a meaningful way, and that is because she is not dedicated to the commitment of the relationship, or to motherhood. As a result, she will continue this downward spiral into more and more of a disconnect, including lying, cheating, and mistreatment for everyone involved.

Change

Nothing in life is permanent. We live in an ever-changing world. Feelings aren't always consistent, relationships aren't always perfect, and things are forever changing because everything in our world is forever vibrating.

Where there is a disconnect, you need to stop and reflect. It is imperative that you begin an open, honest dialogue with yourself about where you are in your life and where you see things going from there on out. The next step is to make a commitment to do what it takes to expose and stop the dishonesty that underlies the disconnect within yourself. Dishonesty and a sense of disconnection go hand in hand. You can never free yourself of mental pain if you keep lying to yourself and others. Self-honesty (truth) is the only power that can shine away dishonesty. Honesty with yourself about who you are and what you expect out of life can only result in a fruitful, rewarding, and fulfilling life.

Dishonesty

This brings me to my second example, one which you will probably see as unfair. But I am saying that while not ideal, it is okay, because an individual has the right to live as they please to a certain extent; where other people aren't involved. You must take responsibility for your own unwillingness to see things the way they are when it involves someone trying to pull the wool over your eyes. Let's say a man is in a committed relationship with a woman. He then explores another relationship with a single woman and now has two women whom he is committed to at the same time. Again, I am in no way using this example to suggest any type of gender-specific tendencies. I am simply saying that, like Lori, the man is not being honest with himself.

I am using this example to showcase yet another set of issues related to dishonesty.

However, we are not exploring *situations* per se; we are exploring the self-dishonesty that the man is experiencing in having power over two women at the same time. Granted, in various cultures having more than one woman or one wife is acceptable. But in our culture it is not—it simply doesn't work. Therefore, I am suggesting that in this situation the man is acting selfishly and deceitfully, to himself and to everyone involved. He has made a conscious decision to be deaf and dumb to his own conscience and to his women's feelings. He may be being perfectly honest with himself. He wants BOTH women. Period! However, he is blind to the pain he is causing in not conforming to the expectations of his culture and the needs of his two women. There are of course myriad factors that give rise to cheating and cheaters. But I think that cheating has mainly to do with not being satisfied within one's self. The gratification that one hopes to achieve in his life somehow doesn't happen in a predictable way. Sometimes women don't seem to love him the way they should. His perception of relationships is flawed and everything a relationship should be is not. While this misunderstanding is in his delusional perception of what a relationship means, ego takes over and irrational solutions occur to cover up the inner turmoil.

Had the man been honest with himself about his level of satisfaction in his relationships—including his relationship to *himself*—he would probably not be with either one of the women. Or maybe he would be with multiple women for all the right reasons and with no need for secrecy—a situation acceptable to all parties involved.

All in all it's about being honest with yourself and not allowing other people to sway you based on the judgments they have passed on you. Just about everything comes into play when we look at our own way, and other people's ways of living their life.

"What really matters" differs from person to person, so the expectations are all different.

The In-between

Some people obviously don't value their life while others seem overly concerned about how they want to live. The only thing you can do is honestly consider your life's goals and values, taking time to be clear about them. If someone doesn't fit into the picture as you had hoped, and over time you're still not satisfied; make a shift immediately, because the level of dissatisfaction with that person is likely to grow, possibly exponentially, and rapidly out of control.

Relationships take up so much of our time and energy! I've found that when we talk about the many experiences life has to offer, most of us say that we've learned the most from the tribulations of relationships, while their more pleasant experiences have been more or less taken for granted, and do not seem as illuminating.

A good way to avoid having the same type of negative experiences over and over again is to gain a better understanding of yourself by digging deep within your core to define the standards, values, and morals that you intend to live by. Be honest with yourself so that honesty and clarity will inform your every experience. I could talk about countless situations, detail by detail, but it's not about the details. You must simply know when it's time to take a step back from the details and see a difficult situation for what it is. In taking that step back, you will usually find that you weren't being honest with yourself and failed to see circumstances for what and how they were.

The way to move beyond and forward in your life is to take life experiences for what they are. Find out what works for you and keep on doing that while also leaving behind all that brings discord to your life. If you live in honesty, you usually have no regrets and your life makes sense. If you live in dishonesty, eventually you cannot keep up with the warring, mismatched fragments which are inevitable when clashing lies come home to roost. Live in honesty so that you can be more in tune with the truth of your being.

Life Experiences and Their Connection to Source

Many times we see misfortune only in the light of victimhood. Yet it is through misfortune that we can find what is most missing in our lives, and that is *courage*. We can analyze our major life experiences from many different angles, but ultimately what remains is a profound understanding and strength within ourselves.

All that happens within us can be truly known only as understanding, understanding that we somehow arrive at ourselves. The clarity of this understanding corresponds directly to our acceptance and connection to Source. Let's say you are in an unfulfilling relationship, and your partner no longer encourages or stimulates your personal growth. He or she is neglectful and unkind to you. One day, seemingly out of the blue, you realize that you are worth much more than your partner's assessment of you, now accepting that you deserve more and, in fact, must get more.

Spirit lives within us. It is always connected to Source, and Source always knows the way to fulfill our worldly mission. Source can intervene in our lives at any time, speaking to us directly to get us back on track. Spirit communicates what needs to happen now. It is through spirit that we understand when we are on track or off track. It is through consciousness that we can formulate the clear thoughts and feelings needed to interpret the messages that Source is giving us.

You don't just suddenly come to understand something within yourself. Source always steps in, connecting to spirit and demanding that consciousness wake up to the truth of the matter right away. Once it is understood that you are in an unfulfilling relationship, for instance, and you acknowledge that your needs are not being met, an epic struggle is likely to ensue. Have you ever heard the saying: You can lead a horse to water but you cannot make him drink? Speaking directly to you, Source nudges you ever closer to the "living waters" of truth and love. But it is up to you to do what you must with that understanding. You are not suddenly abandoned by Source once you are spoken to, but now it's up to you to live your life as you know you should! Source, whom some call "the Father," is indeed like a father who tells his teenage son to buckle up, drive slowly, and not drink and drive. He tells his son only enough to caution him, but ultimately a father lets his son grow into the man that he is becoming. A father may take some precautions for his son, such as installing OnStar in the car for direct access to help, but for the most part, his son is on his own.

Listen to Source

Source is always with us. It has given us spirit as a direct link to Source. Spirit is our OnStar that connects us to Source. Then we must find the strength within to push forward with our dreams. After all, we have come into this world for the purpose of fulfilling a dream. It's important to remember that every life experience has the potential to bring you closer to where you ought to be. Yes, so many terrible and unfair things happen! You are falsely accused, you are mistaken for someone else, you can become very ill, your house may have burned down. . . . You can probably tell me hundreds of ways you've been victimized, but rather than complaining, you should be listening! Listening closely when Source speaks will teach the lessons needed to push you forward.

Sometimes when the momentum has slowed or is lost within ourselves, we are pushed forward by misfortune. Source responds to our troubles at once. It helps us to get back on track, making us leery of the poor choices we'd been repeating in our lives. These choices include unhealthy relationships based on low estimation of our self-worth, resulting in the vicious cycling of the same experiences and circumstances over and over again. The only way to rise above misfortune is to make an emphatic decision to move beyond that experience. Most of us often wait until we are at the end of our rope to take a definite stand, while all along Source has been speaking to us, offering the guidance to help us move forward.

Coming frighteningly close to self-destruction can open our eyes to a profound new understanding and appreciation of life. Chances are, you were supposed to go through that "self-destruct" period only to discover who you truly are. Most times after we awaken from self-ignorance, we are able to truly smile for the first time and truly know what happiness is. Sometimes you discover that you'd been smiling so long for someone else that you never truly knew how to smile for yourself—not until you dropped off the end of that rope.

Why would life lead you through tribulations before you truly understand what it means to smile for the first time? Why would someone put in 20 years of phony smiles before leaving an unfulfilling relationship? And the answer is simple: You wanted to know what it was like to truly smile, to genuinely smile and have it come from your heart. You wanted to fully savor that deep connection within yourself. You may say, I wouldn't have wanted to be in an unfulfilling relationship for 20 years just to learn to smile from my heart! Why would I wish that on myself? To this I would say: 20 years is a small price to pay for a lifetime that can only bring you more real smiles. Going forward, you would be in a much better space to live in harmony and joy. Despite the pain of those 20 years, you've probably accomplished much; maybe you had children, you gained an education and a better understanding of where you are and where you're going.

Back to Source

Life experiences are about finding your way back home, back to Source, back to your inner being, and for you to delight in your blessings. Appreciate all that Source has done for you over the years to keep you on track to your dreams and your desires. Sometimes we attach all our hopes and dreams to the presence of other beings in our life; in their absence, it feels like a struggle to keep moving forward.

One question that I find myself asking is why it's so easy for certain people to have such a huge impact on my life, while others just skim the surface, and others may strike me as insignificant. Source has given us life and plugged us into a destiny that we co-created, and we are one expression of a species that communicates with others. People have a profound influence on our lives. That's just the way it is. Certain individuals can act as teachers for self-discovery. In many cases this is a single person who fails to go away from our lives. In my own experience, this person usually stays around for approximately ten years to act as my teacher of self. This person draws out new self-insights and aspirations. When you no longer need this person in your life, they are usually harmoniously removed from your personal sphere and you move on to who and what is to be your next teacher.

Then there are those who don't have any kind of emotional hold over us. Despite the type of relationship that we have with them, they just don't impact our being very much. This can be a friend or even a confidante—someone whom you're certain you can trust. For most people, the teacher in their life is the person who has the greatest hold over them; everyone else becomes secondary to that person. When you've learned your lesson from the teacher in your life, you find it necessary to let them go. Often life conspires to do this for you.

Many of life's greatest lessons involve self-discovery through discomfort—mental, emotional, and sometimes even physical. While I obviously do not celebrate someone mentally or physically abusing another, the fact remains that we do sometimes experience what is termed "abuse" from the people closest to us. Such extreme situations teach us a great deal about ourselves, and that we have the strength to walk away and never repeat that stance of vulnerability again. If you find that you are very clingy with someone, in most cases you view that person as a teacher in your life. I am not talking about you being possessive of someone.

Possessiveness entails trying to take ownership of someone's life in a manipulative and controlling way, while to be clingy with someone suggests an unhealthily needy desire for that person. There is a very fine line between being clingy and being possessive. In our present-day vernacular, being clingy is considered especially distasteful, but the aspect of clinginess I am looking at works more as an eye-opener to you. It tells you that you are holding on to someone to partake in a learning experience.

Life teaches us constantly. And there are lessons to be learned in everything. Take life one step at a time and accept it just as it is. Keep learning so that you can keep growing and becoming more and more the person you have come here to be.

Cherish each moment and strive for the best. Life gives to you everything that you give to it.

3

Consciousness

Power, Control, Manipulation and Courage

Life can sometimes be about control, power, and manipulation between individuals. This is another great challenge in an individual's life, where one can experience the quality of courage.

True courage transcends control and manipulation. We see this in children all the time as they gain the courage to turn into "their own person" (rather than what their parents have mapped out for them). As you transition into adulthood, the courage you gained in standing up to your parents for your independence suddenly gets tested when you engage with the bullies of the real world.

Life's Bullies

Yes, there are bullies in the real world. Bullies are people who try to break you and keep you down. Most of these people are very close to us, coming in the form of friends, lovers, and colleagues. While you may spend much of your youth mustering up the courage to deal with the only "bullies" that you know—your parents!—That doesn't prepare you for the bullies of the real world. It sometimes takes people a long time to confront their bullies! It can be hard to have a voice when you feel that you've got no more air in your lungs.

People take advantage. Some people want to take as much as they can from you just because they feel empowered to take. This kind of person takes simply because you are giving, and will continue to take all that you've got until your soul is on empty. Unloving people don't need any particular reason to harm you; all they need are unlimited opportunities to take from you. As this is a world of shared energies, some people—popularly known as "psychic vampires"—just feed off the energy of others until their victim is fed up and says *enough is enough!*

Life gives us the courage of will to move beyond all difficulties. It is in this courage that you discover a profound freedom that you never knew existed. So many of us struggle to find the will, the courage, and the strength to confront the bullies in our lives. We sometimes cower behind difficult circumstances to keep ourselves in despair and therefore too weak and afraid for confrontation. We sometimes use "love" as an excuse to keep ourselves subjected to another. For instance: An uneducated man is married to a woman who is financially set, college educated, and well grounded in family values. She talks down to her husband and belittles him in conversation because she has a wide vocabulary and his is limited. He is frivolous with money, and with a weakness for shallow sex with any woman he can find. His behavior is, in part, a way at lashing out at the control that his wife has over him.

These circumstances set the stage for all that is to follow. Both wife and husband misbehave, each treating the other disrespectfully. Slowly and insidiously, they are leeching the very soul from each other by being mean-spirited and deceitful. To understand control, power, and manipulation, you have to realize that they are the products of a person's effort to protect his or her ego.

One cannot control another without knowing that person's weakness. When it comes to control, power, and manipulation, it is all about personally taking something from someone and using that against them. Ill-will and abuse of power can harm both the victim and the perpetrator, which is one reason we have mental institutions, psychiatrists, and therapy to help us when we lose touch with reality.

You may say that power, control, and manipulation are all subjective, and have too many different aspects to discuss under one banner. And I would agree. These dynamics and their effects are all highly subjective, but in this husband-wife example, I cannot make my point without also being subjective.

Unfortunately, life comes with these aggressive forces, and they are with us from birth. The doctor spanks you to make you cry, and the story goes on from there. In every context, power, control, and manipulation are present in life. Things become tricky when someone uses these forces against your well-being, retarding your development. But we can take heart knowing that, through it all, courage is always available to take your life to the next level.

Control

Highly spiritual people, deeply rooted in Source, can control to some extent the inevitable negative inputs of life. Often too, they must forgo some of that control to put their trust in a teacher of some sort, who can assist them in reaching a higher level of spiritual awareness.

Seek to control yourself. Seek to control your own actions and reactions. In the vicissitudes of life we often find ourselves in the position of the oppressed or the oppressor. Sometimes we are acting on both sides of this spectrum. To be in control of your life, you must let go of being the oppressor. As the oppressor, you may feel a sense of perverted pleasure in emotionally dominating someone, but you will surely find that there is no reward in it for you. When the weaker one finds the will and desire to be who they are destined to be, you will certainly see courage arising to balance the situation.

Your Personal IGPS (Internal Guidance Positioning System)

When somebody is aware of their connection to the power of Source, there is no need for the false power of control and manipulation. We all have an IGPS installed within us. This connection is between your spirit and Source. This connection is facilitated by everything life has given you to reconnect with Source. It is your heart, mind, soul, and consciousness.

Your heart tells you if you're feeling good, and lets you know if you're heading the right way or the wrong way. Your mind is essentially how your brain processes information; it tries to interpret and understand this world. Your soul is your spirit and your direct connection to the world of spirit and to the reality of Source. And in your consciousness is your own warehouse of understanding to use in making the appropriate and best choices for the higher good of all.

When you are in total connection with your Source and you are following your IGPS, how would it be possible for someone to control, manipulate, or have power over you? It is totally impossible for someone to have any kind of hold over you when you know where you are going. When you have clear goals and aspirations, it is virtually impossible for someone to keep you from achieving those goals. In football, if a running back is running to score a touchdown, he does everything in his power to avoid being tackled, and keeps running to the end zone as long as he can. That running back is unstoppable once he has an opening and locks in on the end zone.

It's the same with life! You are unstoppable if you know where you're going. In spite of that, when you don't have a clear understanding of where you're going and what you're supposed to be doing, it is easy for people to control, manipulate, and have power over you. Generally, that control doesn't last very long because the strongest human desire—some say even above being loved—is to be *free*. Out of oppression courage is born. When you don't know how to proceed, refrain from getting into situations that would expose your vulnerabilities.

Vulnerability

Vulnerabilities are the particular ways in which you are weak, and ultimately you are responsible for their cause, which is your unawareness of spirit and Source. Vulnerability can occur when consciousness is distracted by itself. What do I mean, you ask? Well, it happens when we consciously ignore our spirit and its directions for fulfilling our purpose; it's like being busy texting while driving a car.

When you text and drive, or talk on your cell phone and drive, you are reducing your reaction time to whatever may be coming up on the road. You give up control and responsibility to the other drivers, thus becoming instantly vulnerable to their own vulnerabilities and aggressions. Your mind is busy attending to something else. Maybe consciousness is so fixed on a fantasy—say, of what will happen when you arrive at your destination—that you can't objectively make proper decisions. For whatever reason, it's not paying attention to the road. There are so many ways you can "lose yourself," and being vulnerable is just one of them. Not understanding your purpose in the world, and never quite figuring out where you fit in the grand scheme of things, are at the root of vulnerability in this thing called life.

Level of Consciousness

There are different levels of consciousness. Consciousness can choose to listen or not to listen. Consciousness has the option of being here now in the present or not being here. Consciousness always has a choice in what it considers and does. What influences our consciousness? Why doesn't it do what it ought to do and just pay attention and follow through with what our IGPS is telling it to do? It is through consciousness that inventions and discoveries are made. It is through consciousness that we can fully explore the stream of energy within us. It is that which allows discoveries to be born and expressed.

Anything that gives you options leaves you open to coming from an empowering side or a vulnerable side. The role of consciousness in life's design is to facilitate the connection between spirit and Source. Disconnection (or what *seems to be* disconnection) doesn't happen often, but consciousness is always ready to bridge the gap. It's similar in a sense to losing one's signal on their cell phone. Dead spots occur. It's just the way life is.

This is the one time our hearts can mislead us, because control, power, and manipulation have an emotional pull on our hearts. Your heart is supposed to lead you to a better, more peaceful place, and to well-being; however, it can be so strung out on love or anger that any type of overwhelming emotional vibration can send mixed messages between heart and soul, and those messages can be misconstrued by consciousness.

This miscommunication between the heart and consciousness can spiral out of control and turn into what I call The Crazy.

The Crazy

Sadly, sometimes The Crazy gets the best of us. It happens at the point when we are at our lowest, and appear to have lost all control over ourselves. The Crazy within is most evident when people reject you. When people don't care to be in your company anymore, The Crazy grabs ahold of you. Your thoughts run out of control. You have no idea who you are and you demand an explanation from others as to what has caused your erratic behavior.

The Crazy sets in when we don't feel valued. And when we don't value or love ourselves enough, we rely on others to assure us of our self-worth. Consciousness begins to narrow, conjuring an illusion that seems very real. In the process, the truth is obscured. The facts of the situation become irrelevant, and all that we know is what we think we know, and what we know is actually nothing.

When we look in the mirror we are so unhappy with the person that we see. We become irate, upset with everything and everyone. Our mood morphs into ongoing dissatisfaction. Nothing and no one can make us feel better. When The Crazy takes hold of you, you are despondent and locked into that mood for what could be a very long time. Sometimes it takes months or even years to move beyond such feelings.

When The Crazy possesses you, it is the most isolating, lonely, and miserable state to be in. We become so isolated and disconnected and out of touch with reality that we miss out on life. Life begins to pass us by. Time flies forward, and if you're not careful, *years can pass by unlived!*

The truth of the matter is that you're the only one suffering during this ordeal. Your craziness has no impact at all on the other person or people involved in the rejection. Your mental state stands alone, powerless in its paralysis. If anything would result from a flare-up of your anger, it would be further rejection and continued avoidance by the rejecter. We are all somehow furtively crazy.

We can all get to a place where we feel helpless. All of us sometimes lose control. We all have moments when we secretly want to jump ship. The irrational within can either break us or make us. Sad to say, it breaks most of us. But if we could only understand that *we ourselves are the actual cause of The Crazy!* We are the only ones pushing craziness to spiral out of control. We allow our minds to take us down that path of no return.

It takes time. It takes self-love. It takes courage to get over and beyond The Crazy within. We have to forgive ourselves for being so unkind, unloving, and unsupportive to our spirit. We have to forgive all the craziness within ourselves before we can move on and beyond it. Living in that state can sow seeds of insecurity and regret. Allowing oneself to fester in the harvest of craziness can be destructive to our soul, inhibiting our progress until we begin anew.

It helps to remember that we are from a loving Source and from an infinite font of happiness. We have to accept rejection when it presents itself to us. We must let it be and release it so that we can move on to the love, joy, and creativity waiting to be born in us.

4

The Keys

The keys are everything that we use to successfully navigate through life. The keys are also everything that we use to bring us into being more of ourselves. They are the instruments that we use to keep us connected to our life mission. One of the most valuable keys opens the way to a shift within and around ourselves through a commitment that we follow. These clues are built into the design of life. Life has given us a Guidance System made up of our heart, soul, mind, and consciousness to find our way. Most, important, life has given us spirit, which is forever and always connected to Source. These paths are always available to us, because we are always connected to Source through spirit. All along, the formula to our happiness is within us.

Key of Time

Time is forever moving forward. Time constantly reminds us of our desire to progress, because as time moves forward, so should we. Time is the springboard and momentum of life's design. It gives us the opportunity to be self-aware, to move from Point A to Point B to Point C, thereby fulfilling our destinies and ultimately returning to Source, where other streams of energy get their chance to come into being.

This is why you have to make good use of your time. You have to maximize the usefulness of your time. You have to make sure that you are focused on you in this lifetime because, chances are, all you have is one shot to make it worth your while.

Key of Inspiration

Inspiration is essential to life's design. Life gives you infinite sources of inspiration. Inspiration, like energy, is neither created nor destroyed. Inspiration cannot be taken away from you, no matter what. Academic achievement, financial status, ethnicity, even religious affiliation—none of that matters when it comes to inspiration.

Life has given you the gift of inspiration to carry out and fulfill your dreams. Yes, externals can trigger your inspiration, making you more aware of who you need to be, but inspiration is already inside of you. Regardless of what has sparked your inspiration, that inspiration was inevitably going to manifest in your life.

Finding the key to inspiration is simple, and easy to recognize when you have it. You will feel it in quietness, self-honesty, persistence, asking, and giving of yourself, all of which bring happiness.

The Key of Silence

Life has given you the gift of silence, wherein inspiration abides and is known through stillness, and quieting of the mind. Life has made us so perfect that we can shut our minds off at any given time and speak directly to Source. Quietness is a direct route to the opening of inspiration. It is in our most still moments that we truly see things, and clarity is ours.

Self-Honesty

Self-honesty is clearer and deeper when we quiet our minds. Self-honesty can take you deep within your purpose in this existence. When you are honest with yourself about your fears, goals, and your most private thoughts, a shift begins to take place within yourself. And it is in this shift that doors within your consciousness begin to open. This shift starts to break down walls within self. Your attitude is transformed. You become more receptive and calmer. You are more relaxed and a bit more patient.

As your attitude changes, you begin to feel better about yourself. You appear to be glowing, inwardly and outwardly. People begin to respond to you differently. Life begins to transform for you. This transformation is priceless! Life has already given you the devices for transformation. It has given you a heart, a mind, consciousness, and all that is needed to be honest with yourself. And best of all, neither level of education, nor social status, nor ethnicity prevents you from accessing the truths that life has given you to be happy.

Persistence is another tool for self-refinement and realization of our goals. Persistence is our will and desire to strive for something. Our dedication, our passion, our yearning for more of life have already given us quality to make it through this existence.

Do you see how you are the only person who stands between yourself and your goals? Do you understand that life has already given you all that you need within yourself to make this lifetime everything that you want it to be?

Happiness

Shifting within yourself continues throughout your development. You should always welcome these shifts as opportunities to reconnect to Source. Powerful and rejuvenating, these deep inner changes point you in the best direction for fulfilling your destiny.

The remedy to life rests within oneself, and not in another. Although you may love your children, they do not hold the key to your sanctuary; nor do you hold the answers to theirs. Although you love and are committed to another person, they are not your refuge, either. You may, in fact, easily mistake anything or anyone as your "be all, end all," but the true explanation is within the self. The passport to happiness sometimes waits upon time. With the passage of time comes experience, and with experience come greater opportunities and greater facility in the use of this "key." This of course brings us back to the Big Question: What is the meaning of life for an individual?

Self-Reflection

Self-reflection should be accessed all the time. Self-reflection keeps our eyes focused on ourselves and what we should be doing. It encourages us to take a loving, more caring approach to our situation and circumstances, while at the same time discouraging us from judging others, and speaking unlovingly to (and of) them.

As you reflect on yourself, you must be honest with yourself. You must also be patient, allowing time to pass without having all the "answers," and ever open to inspiration. Self-reflection is critical in determining where you're coming from and where you're going.

Although life is always moving forward, somehow most of us get stuck in inertia. We turn around and, ten years down the road, notice that we are the same weight, in the same job, in the same space with the same relationships, and everything seems, for the most part, pretty much the same as ever. Meanwhile, everything outside of us appears to be much more dynamic! Other people's lives keep developing; everything else just seems to be more "happening" for everyone else but us.

We are alive, but not really *alive!* We are here, but not really here! We are one amongst many, a cog in the wheel. We have to forget about everybody else. Forget about all the circumstances, forget about the past. Just know that right now, it's just you—you're the only one in the race.

So what do you do? I once heard that you are truly yourself when no one else is looking. If we look at our life in this way—that we are here and here alone—we can then see that the monsters we are fighting are truly the obstacles that we put in our own way. We stay in relationships that aren't benefiting us, and we are impatient when we need to be patient. We inhibit ourselves from truly living. These are things we do to ourselves.

Inspiration

The way is in inspiration. Seek to discover revelations within yourself, and worlds open up within you. Search to find things that bring you joy. Search for that which makes you exceptional, so that an action can encourage a desperately needed change within yourself. When I talk about action, I am not talking about things that make you react hastily, out of suddenly felt urgency. I am talking about a conscious effort to act in ways that promote permanent change within your life. If you love singing, start singing, and take the steps needed to sing. Join a chorus or take singing lessons. These are steps that all but ensure a permanent, lasting change. If you know there is something you wish to learn, find a way to take small steps in that direction; even just talking and thinking about it can inspire change. The possibilities would begin to open up for you from then on.

You can access the secret by becoming quiet and still. You can meditate and know the Oneness with your inner self. Self-honesty is also important when accessing the answer to yourself. For a pure connection to Source, you have to be able to fess up all dishonesty. You have to be persistent and consistent in your practice when connecting to Source. Then and only then can you ask in your purest state of mind for that connection to manifest things and situations that are for the highest good of all.

You have to accept where you are in your life in the here and now. Accept that you are where you are. Don't blame anyone, not even yourself, for where life has taken you. Just accept the position that you are in. Recognize where you are. Understand the difference between where you were and where you are going, for it is only then that you can make a shift.

In life science, enzymes aid chemical reactions so that a result can occur. An enzyme works to trigger or speed a specific reaction. Just as in biology we rely on our enzymatic helpers to get things moving, so too in our lives does perfectly orchestrated assistance appear in the form of a teacher, a friend, a book, or whatever. You feel a personal connection with this blessing that has come to show you the path that you hold within.

People

To access the keys to your life you need people. People who have a deep love and appreciation for you and who want to see you succeed are the "keys" I refer to. Don't ever assume that only the people you surround yourself with can care about you. Sometimes the people in our immediate vicinity—front and center in our lives—are not fruitful in their thoughts for us, and would rather see us fail than succeed.

Seek counsel in a mentor, a pastor, an uncle, an aunt, a trusted neighbor. Naturally, you will be able to discern who has a genuine care for you and who does not by their actions and words.

If someone ridicules you in any way, and disregards your thoughts and feelings, that person cares very little for you. If a person cannot see much good in you, that person is obviously not in sync with you. If a person can only criticize you (no matter how subtly!), he or she doesn't have much faith in you and is therefore not mentor material!

Find and seek out people who genuinely laugh and smile with you. Seek out people who will comfort you in your times of need. Seek out people who attentively listen to you, and provide you with thoughtful advice. Seek out people who can help you think objectively and critically about your situations. Seek out those who are secure in their own skin. Surround yourself with people who have no ulterior motives, and simply want to be your true friend. And above all, find people who want to see you achieve your goals, and will help you to realize the endless possibilities within yourself. It's always encouraging to speak to someone who lifts your spirit! Remember, it is relatively easy to find someone who will cry with you, but not so easy to find the friend who will *rejoice* when you win the state lottery!

Additional implements you can use to expand your vision and possibilities are books, DVDs, and inspirational lectures. These can serve you a great deal in getting you inspired and thinking about your life. While books usually cannot speak directly to your particular situation, they can speak to you in a general way, providing direction amidst the confusion. Books are great for showing you the various possibilities; they can invigorate you endlessly, changing you. Find time to go to the library, the bookstore, or ask someone if they have a good book to help you on your journey.

"A good book" may for you turn out to be *The* Good Book, the Bible, or various other ancient scriptures. Biblical scripture can be very inspirational and can uplift your spirit. The Bible is loaded with wisdom, which may be embraced through a religion or Bible study group. Be wary of cults and other groups that use faith in a guru to get people to "join up." I am very emphatic in suggesting that you join a practice or a church to learn the Word and works of God for inspiration. Be conscious and careful about what you join to learn about faith and spiritual works. The Bible, although wide open to interpretation, can be very inspirational when you reach your own personal understanding of its messages. Make sure that you are in control of you before joining any practice or religion to learn about God, the Bible, or other holy books.

Spirituality

Spirituality is essential for inspiration. Seeking a relationship with your higher self, the god within you, can channel rewarding positive energy into your heart and soul. Spirituality involves opening to spirit. Faith is a meaningful way of awakening your spirit and it can have an inspirational, everlasting effect on your soul. Relationship with your higher source energy, the Maker, is the only truly powerful connection. In a heartbeat, your spirit can experience an everlasting transformation. There are many paths we can take to connect with the spiritual side of ourselves, including church, temple, mosque, the Bible, the Koran, and the works and practices of Hinduism and Buddhism, to name but a few.

Pray

For now, you can begin by praying! Praying is almost universal, no matter what religion you may embrace. It's a great way to connect and shift within the spirit. You have two options when trying to open to a shift within spirit: you can use religion to guide your spiritual quest, or you can hold fast to your principles and connect to your higher self.

How do I pray, and to whom am I praying? The force within you is the spirit. Open to the universe and to Source by closing your eyes and connecting with the darkness. Ask that the force within will guide you (intuition), and, without self-resistance, allow that shift to occur. Ask for the medium that you should use to strengthen your spiritual force to that which is more loving, more truthful, more beautiful.

Your spirit lives in you. Spiritual fulfillment can seem to come about from religion, or a practice, but your spirit lies within you, so spiritual fulfillment can only come from you. It is when you are most at peace with yourself; when you pray or speak to your soul that spiritual fulfillment comes over you. If you look at a baby just smiling and laughing for no particular reason, you notice that they are in full connection with their spirit. In order to relocate that smile and that natural laughter that you once also had, you must seek it out. That's because you've become so consumed with so much of life that you're not in conscious connection with your spirit.

But spirit always reminds us that it is there, especially when we most need the reminder! And it is in that chuckle we have to ourselves when reflecting on a memory, and in that intuitive smile that just spreads across our face when we're alone. It's the untroubled baby in us that comes out; it's the unbreakable connection to Source that reminds us that we are always and forever children of the universe.

In praying, it is only natural that you laugh, smile, cry, and reconnect to the lost part of your soul. A baby laughing and smiling isn't looking for recognition, because a baby's self-joy is enough to fulfill its soul. Laugh, smile, and connect with others; let them see your radiant light, but don't look for anything in return.

So what do I say when I am praying? I close my eyes and say thank you for inspiring me to smile again, thank you for enabling me to cry, thank you for allowing me to feel whole again. Thank you for completing me. Thank you for living in me. And the rest will come naturally.

Giving

The last point that I want to emphasize is giving. Giving is such an empowering, rewarding, selfless experience! Giving changes your vibrational alignment, but only when you give wholeheartedly. If you give from the depths of your heart you experience peace and inspiration. In giving naturally you feel good, you smile more, and you know that you've done your best. Giving inspires you to give in ways you never could have imagined possible. But, you should only give when it feels natural and heartfelt.

I remember several times when I couldn't finish my meal in restaurants, and everything had been so delicious that I had it bagged to go. But before I could reach home someone would be standing outside hungry and in need of my assistance, so I would gladly hand over my food. While that meal had cost me a pretty penny and I was really looking forward to the leftovers, I found it only natural and within my heart to give what I could. This may not be an extraordinary example of giving, but at the time that's the best I could do, and while I give to charity and run for charitable causes, I rather mention the simpler ways that I give.

Of course, we all give differently. I encourage you to find room within your soul and within your heart to start small and give a little—even if it's as little as offering your newspaper to someone else instead of throwing the paper away. And if no one wants it, you can make a point of recycling it. Most people have many opportunities to give within their families as well. It can be as little as a phone call to check up on someone who is ill or just lonely, or an encouraging card, just because you want to put a smile on someone's face. Look for ways to give naturally. New possibilities for giving are sure to turn up, encouraging you to grow in generosity.

Consciousness

What makes us turn around and decide to change our life while others are stuck in the same La-Z-Boy all their lives? What makes us follow our IGPS? What is this inner IGPS, anyway? Who are the other drivers in this game of life, and are they also connected to their own inner self?

Consciousness is what gave and continues to give life to us. Some say that it is life. We can at least agree that it is fundamental to life's design. What a privilege it is that we can think independently, and act accordingly! Your consciousness is what makes you, you. It's that understanding between spirit, Source, and brain.

Consciousness may also be seen as what lies between the brain and its understanding of where one sees herself in this world. Consciousness often seems to operate automatically, and I'm not just referring to all of our out-of-sight bodily processes! Have you ever noticed that when you're writing something, your thoughts are going faster than the speed of your pen, and you kind of have to tell your mind to slow down? You have to make a conscious effort to have the words and the writing keep up with each other. You actually have to say, word by word, what you're writing or else you won't be able to keep up.

Consciousness can be so fast that you have to use your brain to keep up with it. It can also appear as infinite slowness, the all-here-now-ness that's not going anywhere because it is everywhere!

What happens when a person suffers from a psychological disorder? What happens to a person who is, to one degree or another, out of sync with consciousness? Some kind of miscommunication is going on between the brain and the mind, and they are no longer working together harmoniously. Substance abuse, dysfunctional environment, ignored IGPS System, and, on rare occasion, "bad genes" can all contribute to these very difficult challenges. It's good to remember, though, that <u>within</u>

consciousness is all possibility, so that no one should ever be "written off."

We are made from perfection. Many things happen in the living of our life that make us become increasingly *human* beings. We are so delicate that anything can happen. That's why we have to hold our babies with care. Just like them, we are all very delicate, very vulnerable, and the difficulties we encounter can actually wear out the "wiring" in our connection to our IGPS.

I don't think life is as careless as an automobile manufacturer, but I do think that life is very delicate and the connections in some of its design can be weak.

Whether these weak links were co-created or not, I wouldn't know. I cannot know what someone else co-created.

I was a premature baby. I was born in the seventh month of my mother's pregnancy. Just barely viable, I could hardly wait to come out and start my life. I had to be incubated until I developed sufficiently to safely go home. I weighed in at 4 pounds 7 ounces at birth. Was my premature birth a part of my design to be born so early and risk my life? I would say yes. I think I co-created my premature birth to see if I could survive, and then, surviving, know myself as a true "survivor." I see it as all part of a plan to "put myself out there" so that I'd know that it is okay to risk everything like that—as I am doing right now in writing this book. Luckily for me, Source made sure that there were doctors and the health care needed for me to "make it." Still, I needed the help of other humans to grow. Although my baby consciousness appeared not to know what it was doing, my spirit, ever connected to Source, informed that consciousness, and all those around me, with all that was needed for me to live.

Consciousness is alive and with us even in the womb. When a child is under age one and starts making sounds that he believes comprise a conversation with you, you know it is consciousness, longing to express in that child. That connection between brain and mind are present, but we have to teach them our language. We have to give them words to express that consciousness.

The way I see it, mental disorders could have been co-created, perhaps to express conscious rebellion against spirit and Source. In any case, the design of life is perfect. Life couldn't be life if it were not perfect. But it's the manmade details of life that we get hung up on. It's the details that cause us to suffer and speculate.

Asking

If you don't know something, you should ask! Asking is one of the most critical ways to a rewarding life. In asking, you receive—it's as simple as that. In asking, you free self-consciousness from overindulging in itself. Do you remember as a child when you asked your parent for another cookie after you'd already had dessert? You were probably a little anxious, because you knew that they could probably say no, and most likely they did say no because you already had dessert. But sometimes you got lucky and they said "Okay, have another cookie, but let it be your last for the night." From childhood on, one of two things can happen when you ask: you get what you're asking for the first time around or you get it the second time around. One way or another, you get what you ask for. It may not come wrapped in the pretty package you'd envisioned, but it comes, nonetheless.

Asking frees you from the non-specificity of consciousness. And, because we are all made of the same stuff, we can be of assistance to each other. Yes, we may have come here to fulfill our own intentions, but we have each other for support. For example: Say you're driving to Canada from the United States and you're confused by the directions that you downloaded from the Internet. Don't you feel much more at ease when you ask for directions and gain a better understanding of where you're going? So much of our potential is stifled by our own narrow self-consciousness that is too timid to even ask for directions! This is a major reason why so many couples are in unfulfilling relationships; neither party cares enough, or is skillful enough, to ask the other person what their intentions are for the relationship. Unable or unwilling to clarify their desires and expectations, both people involved in the relationship are simply waiting for the other person to react. What you then experience are reactions, reacting to reactions, in a vicious circle of meaninglessness.

Asking for direction (guidance) on your journey of life can reduce the uncertainty that comes with taking any journey. You have to learn to ask the right questions of the right people so you can get truly helpful clarification. You have to become so aware of what's on your life map that the right questions come naturally. You might say, "May I have a cookie, please?" And you would probably get a cookie because you see it and it's available for you to have. An ungracious or unfocused "Where is my cookie?" would probably not yield the cookie! The response to that would be more along the unsatisfying lines of: "You have no cookie? Did you lose your cookie? When did you buy the cookie?" Now I know you aren't reading this book for instruction on the proper ways to ask for a cookie. Yet there is a lesson to be learned in asking for anything, including a cookie. It is that you have to know how to ask the right questions so you can get what you want, and politely asking is always the way to start.

I know you want to know how to ask the right questions on your journey of life, and you also want to know whom you should be addressing these questions to. So, how do you ask for something and get what you're asking for? Well, you have to really want what you're asking for! *You have to feel what you want.* You have to know and feel what it would be like to have that thing already. For instance, you may ask, "When am I going to meet the right man?" But the question was stated incorrectly! The question should have been, "Where am I going to meet the right man, and what do I have to do to put myself in the position of meeting this man?" Wanting this man and having this man should feel the same.

I don't know exactly why this should be so, but it seems to me that men enjoy a stronger likelihood of feeling and already having what they desire. Of course, it doesn't matter what sex you are, as anybody can learn to experience the feeling of desiring something and already having it. But I am still convinced that men, more than women, have refined the art of imagery. And why? In our patriarchal system, men had centuries to capitalize on the opportunity to realize the coinciding of desiring and having. Whether this manipulation of consciousness is learned behavior or instinctive, it seems that more men than women are "good at" creative visualization.

In any case, you have to admit that men and women are very different. And we certainly have enough books out there, trying to explain why "men are from Mars and women are from Venus," but that appears to be pretty much all we know, give or take a few hormones.

I want to be sure that I have explicitly explained the dynamics of how when you really want something, you have to desire it and feel as if you already have it. This surefire way of manipulating energy is a great way of getting what you want. Whether what you're asking for is good for you or bad is beside the point, though I'll speak about it later on in this chapter.

The point is that you have to ardently desire what you're asking for and you have to ask spirit; your spirit will connect to Source and make whatever it is you're asking for come to pass.

Lest you are thinking that this ask-and-receive formula is a promise to you, I should also tell you that this dynamic is not like Rhonda Byrne's *The Secret. The Secret,* as you probably know, is a book about the law of attraction and getting everything you want. But I'm not talking about the law of attraction when I say, as did Jesus Christ, "Ask, and you shall receive." I'm talking about asking for what you want in the purest of expressions, fully desiring it, and connecting to spirit and Source to see if it's a part of your life's purpose.

If what you're asking for isn't part of the plan of your existence, chances are it's not going to show up, no matter how much you ask for it. For example: A baby is born with a rare genetic disorder that has resulted in him having no arms and no legs. The fact is, no matter how fervently that child asks for limbs, he isn't going to grow any. I use this example because for a child to ask for arms and legs is the purest of all forms of asking. A child, especially a toddler, has no ulterior motive for having arms and legs other than to be like the others in his family, all of whom have limbs.

This child in his co-creation created a purpose that, chances are, revolved around this handicap. What I am suggesting is that when we ask our spirit a question, Source always responds. Whether it's a response that you want to hear or not, you'll get a reply every time. It's a lot easier to think about asking for a cookie than asking for some limbs. When you asked your parents for another cookie after you'd already eaten dessert, whether you get the reaction you're looking for or not, you're going to get a result.

Asking and Not Receiving

This consideration of *asking* inspires me to talk a bit more about rejection. I know I spoke about it in the previous section, but it warrants a deeper look as part of the plan. Rejection is a part of life's design to get you headed in the direction of where you should be going. If you honestly reflect on all the times you've been involved in a rejection situation, aren't you glad, looking back, that rejection was a part of the plan? Without your being rejected, you wouldn't have ended up in the far better situation you're in now.

When you are rejected be thankful, not sad. Suppose you are headed to Florida from New York City, and you're traveling along Route 95 North. Catching you speeding, a cop pulls you over to issue you a summons for driving at 72 in a 60-mile-per-hour zone. He asks you why you were in such a big hurry, and you tell him you have a long drive ahead of you as you're eager to catch the rays in Florida. The officer looks at you incredulously and says, "You're going the wrong way, ma'am! You should be on 95 South if you expect to get to Florida. You won't catch many rays here in Connecticut in December!" Wouldn't you be thankful that the cop intervened and pointed you in the right direction? I sure would be!

Rejection is just one of the navigational gears that life uses. It need never be taken as a personal attack on you or on your abilities. Rejection is just a tool to keep you on track to fulfilling your life's purpose.

However, your ego can and does have a field day with you, making you think that rejection is a personal attack and that you should do something about it! That's how your individual consciousness messes with you, distracting you from paying attention to your IGPS.

You must understand that there are many levels of consciousness, and if you get caught up in its pettier and ultimately meaningless expressions, it will take you for a lifelong ride. You'll end up so "bewitched, bothered, and bewildered" that before you know it, you'll be totally off course. Human consciousness, as I'll discuss later, makes every effort to be independent of spirit and Source, so it easily takes you on an unwilling joy ride, all the while convincing you that your IGPS is broken. Consciousness attached to an individual ego is not connected to divine purpose; its only interest is in being interested in itself. That's why it's so important to learn to tame your mind.

The workings of your mind are of course essential in fulfilling your purpose. I'll touch on this concept later, but accept for now that you have to be able to tame your mind so that you can ultimately connect to your IGPS and get to where you're going in this life. Try to recognize when you've allowed your thinking to run amok on you, and figure out a way to control it. Without mental activity you would of course be unconscious, so being conscious is good, but controlling what consciousness houses and builds upon can be hard. Accept that some days you'll just have to let your thinking run its course and tire itself out before you can quiet your mind and get it back on track.

Human consciousness can act like a knuckleheaded teenager. That is, it tends to be juvenile and self-centered. Sometimes you almost want to question whether a teenager has a brain, but you know the only explanation for their erratic behavior has got to be their rapidly changing bodies and surging hormones. But never mind how a teenager behaves—you need your knuckleheaded teenager! You need him to get the groceries out of the car; you need him to baby-sit his little brother; you need him to cut the lawn. And most of all, you need him to keep you smiling.

Yes, the human mind is certainly silly at times, and thank heavens for that—it keeps you laughing and smiling at yourself. I know I laugh at myself frequently, and essentially I know that I am laughing at my overactive mind. For example: I'll be in bed, exhausted, trying to go to sleep, while my conscious mind is still so excited by an idea I was working on earlier in the evening that, with no regard for my exhaustion, it gets me out of bed and back to the computer. At times like this I usually laugh at myself and say, "Hey, Karissa! What are you doing? You're exhausted. . . . You can barely move and you want to get out of bed?" But then I'll relent and say, "Okay, you can go on the computer, but after that one idea is put into Photoshop, that's it—back to bed we go."

We all have moments like these when we have to let our consciousness do what it does best when it's inspired. I generally embrace the workings of my mind rather than resist and do battle with it. I much prefer to go with the flow of my consciousness and encounter the ideas that are intriguing or troubling me, because battling with my consciousness will never do any good. I'll never be "over it" fully until I explore it. I'll have to respond to that same call again the next day, or the day after that, until that inspiration or dilemma is understood, embellished, or put to rest.

You may not have realized this awareness within yourself, or taken the time to sit down and become acquainted with your consciousness. After all, you and the contents of your mind are a team, and need to work in harmony to get things done on your journey. If you let your thoughts run wild and get the best of you, you can end up paying a hefty price. If you passively allow your consciousness to play psychological games with you, suggesting that, to find peace, you must eat uncontrollably throughout the night, you will probably gain an immense amount of weight while also increasing the probability of indigestion and heartburn. And you'll be more likely to have a heart attack and or stoke.

You have to find a way to balance your desires and allow them their freedom to express at times; other times, using your IGPS rigidly can only lead to resistance, so being too rigid in your thinking will not result in anything good.

It is, of course, through consciousness that you make all decisions. This "inner voice" directs even the most mundane of decisions: you go to the restroom when your bladder is full. But sometimes there's a conflict, because another part of you doesn't want to stop what you're busy doing. Let's say you've gone to a movie and it's just your luck that it turns out to be three and a half hours long. So you buy the super-size drink and jumbo popcorn, nestle into your seat, and proceed to down the entire drink. An hour into the movie and—surprise! You realize that you have to "go." Now if you leave it up to the less mature aspect of consciousness, you'll take a chance and wait till the movie is over to use the restroom for fear of missing an important part of the film. But the "higher" aspect of your consciousness, seeing the fuller picture, cries out that no matter how focused you may be on the movie, *your bladder is full!* That consciousness alerts your imagination: You may urinate on the seat! Whoever cleans the soggy cushion will suffer, and all because of you! What's more, your clothes will be drenched—possibly ruined!—and you will reek! Your date will keep his distance, losing all amorous inclinations! Even if you manage to "hold it," you'll probably get abdominal cramps. So you put immediate gratification aside and go to the restroom. Nothing horrible has happened, and now you can get back to enjoying the show.

Consciousness animates all of us. It can be a voice that laughs when we cry, a person who makes us smile when we don't want to, or someone we don't listen to who orders us to put down that piece of cake. Get to know that energy inside of you. It knows how to truly make you happy.

5

The Power within the Self

The self is so magnificent! When we come to understand and know that we are godly because we are an indispensable part of God that comes directly from God, everything in life begins to make sense, and we know and celebrate the self as something majestic. I use the word God here to mean that which is more than we can understand.

When I talk about being a vessel of God himself, which makes us little gods, I am not making a religious statement to suggest that there is a God. It is simply the only word in our vernacular that suggests something more or higher than the self, perhaps something even bigger than Source. One of the best ways to understand the self as a supernatural entity is to use the word God to name the unnamable originator of this physical design that carries our soul.

The power of our thoughts, the emotions that drive us, the soul within our body—all comprise an energy field with no limits, no boundaries, none of anything preventing this self from being something great. You may say to yourself, I'm not as talented as, I can't sing as well as, I can't run as fast as, and the list of limitations goes on. But it is undeniable that the power within the self is so strong that we cannot hold back from expressing its magnificence.

This Source I speak of is as others have termed it, Source energy. By Source energy, I mean the connection between the self and the Higher Self, and how strong the relationship is between the two. We are always connected to Source! We are only unaware of it (to varying degrees).

The relationship of self to Source is very important in determining the balance of power. How much control are you willing to surrender to your Source energy, and how much of that energy do you control yourself? How much do you believe that your life is in the hands of something more than you, like a God perhaps?

The Mind

The self is not to be misinterpreted or confused with the mind. The self is the soul of you. It is the core of you. The mind is not to be mixed up to mean yourself, as the mind is dependent upon learned behaviors along with a subjective outlook. The mind is constantly in chaos and is always changing and turning and developing into what we call our understanding of our selves and its relationship to the world.

The mind is just a part of what makes us live in flesh. We could not live in this body if we did not have a mind. The mind controls our fleshly body; it gives us an opportunity to really develop and understand our relationship with our self, and to our soul. Maybe in the next dimension, which is the afterlife, that understanding of our self or our soul will ease our entry into that dimension.

Why, you may ask, is the relationship to the self so important in this lifetime? And you may say, babies die, people in other countries aren't as fortunate we are in America. Does everyone have the same right to self-fulfillment? The result is, absolutely. All have the same *right,* but not all have the same access.

The definition of self-fulfillment differs for everyone, regardless of how old you are, or where you come from. A baby's self-fulfillment could have been just to breathe and that was it, and so the baby passes away. Another's self-fulfillment could have been to become a successful business owner, and so it was done.

The thing about life is that you just don't know what is lurking behind that smile, that frown, that facade of someone else. You just don't know what that person's habitual thoughts are. This makes it difficult for me to explain how powerful the self could be, because we all have different missions.

We all have different kinds of expectations, goals, and passions. You might say you just don't have a clue about where you are or where you're going in your life, and you just want things to start making sense before you start losing your mind in this unknown state that we seem to be in.

Unknown

That space of the unknown is very uncomfortable for anyone who hasn't yet discovered his or her purpose in life or what is needed for self-fulfillment. But this unknowingness is the channel from the unknown to the known, and in itself is a kind of clarity.

Being in a state of unknowing is the only way to understanding. Unknowing is when you truly let go of your mind and its control over you. That is, it is when you sincerely say, "Well, what is meant to be, will be." The secret to this is time. Time is the progression of thoughts. Your thoughts can become clearer as time passes. The more time you have to mull them over, the clearer your thoughts become. Eventually, you leave the unknowingness behind and enter into an understanding of something you didn't know before.

How do you understand the Divinity that exists within yourself? How do you make sense of the so-called "mystical experience?"

How do you truly comprehend the intricate design of life? Most of us drive cars, and everyone has at least seen a car, so to help you understand my points I am going to use the automobile as metaphor.

Life's Design

What is life's design? It starts with co-creation in the nonexistence, or void. Let's pretend life is predetermined. In accepting your life as the way it is, allows you the freedom needed to enjoy your existence. You are granted choices as to how you will play out this destined experience. You can express as an animal, a plant, or a human. At this point just accept that it's a choice you've made to exist as a human. Life's design is such that our journey is guided by spirit. In death, the spirit leaves the body and goes back to the realm of nonexistence. When we see bodies that are no longer living, it is obvious to all that the person is utterly "gone." Spirit is what had given them a nice rosy skin color. In death, the vacated body turns pale and blue, leaving no doubt that spirit has left the body.

Everything that spirit is, is life. Life is the connection between you and spirit. Spirit is the fuel of life's design. When oil drains out of a car, everything shuts down, even if the car has gas. Without oil, the engine can explode, after which you can either get a new engine or a refurbished one. When blockage in the heart occurs, and doctors can still save the body, that person will go on living as long as spirit is present.

Life is always connected to Source, and spirit and Source are in constant communication. Spirit is like a battery that life gives us. When the energy of the battery runs out, life expires. If you don't keep the conditions surrounding a battery in good shape, that can also cause a battery to corrode and fail. It's the same with life: if we don't keep our bodies healthy and in good enough condition to house spirit, that can cause spirit to "run out."

How do we experience the connection between Source and spirit? The connection is seen as guidance. It's as if we were plugged into Source to get back on track to purpose and self-fulfillment. Because we have come into being from Source, I use Source and life interchangeably, but they are one and the same.

Spirit is independent of flesh and can plug into Source for information to get us where we need to be. Spirit and body can work in unison to fulfill the purpose that is within each of us. That's why we need spirit, and our mind helps us interpret what spirit means.

It's like having a satellite in space that helps our navigation system tell us where we're going. Spirit, and its relationship to Source, comes to mind. You have the navigation lady speaking the directions through the navigational system—that's our mind, fully connected with and working with Source to get us to our destination. But then you have us humans (resistance within), that calls the navigation girl crazy as we go our own way and end up lost. People call that the ego. However, I know that to be disconnection. When we are not in connection with Source it's a disconnect. I've come to understand the ego as a part of your intellectual self that life has given us to navigate through this existence when we have to be independent of our IGPS.

EGO

Ego overpowers the operation of the self. But in the intricate design of life, we were given the brain to comprehend the link between spirit and Source. So, the ego would then be a malfunction in the intricate design of life.

Life is too clever to have malfunction as a standard part of its design. Ego is a disconnect between Source and spirit that causes us to not stray from the clear-cut directions of our IGPS. It's like coming into a dead zone. Sometimes in a parking lot your satellite navigation system doesn't work and your navigation system is all out of whack. It's the same with the disconnect that happens with life. When the spirit is not in communion with Source, it throws off our IGPS for a second until it reconnects and gets back on track.

To call this disconnect your alter ego, or your ego, is a bit problematic to me because it's simply a disconnect between spirit and Source. The direction and the destination are still very much on track. Your IGPS doesn't shut down; it's simply a lost signal. This is why we need a little bit of help from the brain to know its purpose, so that when a dead zone comes up at least it's unnoticeable. I don't think there are that many dead zones between spirit and Source. I think life's design is far more sophisticated than we think. It is not a part of life's design to have ego play a central part in our lives.

Anything is liable to happen in disconnection from Source, especially when it's left to us to discern the directions and to make appropriate decisions at the moment of disconnection. Ego is there to serve as a way to assist the brain to help with the plan at hand. You type into your navigation system that you're going from east to west. But as your trip begins, you notice a huge pothole. What do you do? You process the hole and determine that you will dodge all future potholes. It is only because we have an intelligent brain that ego is used to help in the decision-making process.

As it turns out, the detours and roadblocks of life are actually there to help us get to where we need to be in life. But to successfully navigate those potholes (the dead zones of Source and spirit), we need an ego and even an alter ego. Without them, we could just run over those "holes" and risk our physical bodies or compromise alignment, with Source. We use our brains to steer the car out of harm's way.

Disconnect

Disconnect doesn't always mean a breaking away from Source, or a dead zone. Sometimes the brain disconnects from the spirit, and it is in that separation that we are confused and off track. Getting back to our navigation system analogy: Source is satellite, spirit is the built-in Guidance System, and the computer speaking directions is our brain. Our being is also in the car, and can choose to either follow all the directions or get caught up in singing along to the radio and missing our turns. However, our IGPS is always there to put us back on track, if only we will listen.

I know I've mentioned resistance several times throughout this book, but it bears repeating. Resistance is a significant force within the self. It is another form of disconnection that is generated by you, the driver of your vessel. Consciousness is that connection between brain and spirit and Source. The GPS of life cannot be turned off. It's up to the driver to listen to that GPS or ignore it, but the more you listen the closer you'll come to reaching your destination. This is the overarching purpose that you co-created with Source in your mission to Earth. If you don't listen, you'll miss your exits and entrances! Then you'll be forced to detour, and the more back roads you must take, the more mazes you'll have to figure out before getting back on course.

"Getting lost" or sidetracked in this way may leave one feeling disconnected, but in fact it's the best route back to spirit and back to Source. Even if you had to take a back road that was bumpy, dark, and narrow to get you back on track, that's just what life will do for you. It awakens your connection to Source, leading to your life's purpose and, ultimately, to self-fulfillment.

But could disconnection mean an actual *split*? Can consciousness override the navigation system? Yes, because your getting lost would be deliberate; essentially, you would have chosen to ignore the instructions of the GPS, careening down the path to self-destruction.

Of course, you do hear people say, "I've found myself again. I don't know what happened, and I can hardly believe I was so long gone." What happens here is the GPS keeps going. Regardless of whether you obey the GPS or not, you may fortuitously come across a new route that puts you back on track. Sometimes Route 85 can take you to Route 95, where they merge. Consciousness operates like this as well. You simply take the ramp to get back on track. Sometimes we seek the entrance ramp to Source, but no matter what we do, going east on 80 or going west on 80 will never put us where we need to be. You have to literally turn around and go back.

Turn Around

Sometimes in life you have to turn around in order to get back on track. That is also a conscious decision, and as soon as you turn around, your IGPS responds happily. However far you may be from your destination, you feel confident that you'll eventually get there. Let's hope at this point that you'll actually have time to make it to where you're going.

The power within is unchanging, everlasting, and always good enough to lead to fulfillment of your destiny. When you fail to listen to your GPS you can waste time and retard your hard-won process of growth and self-discovery. Life's design is very intricate: we were given a brain, spirit, and a direct connection to Source. We use consciousness to get us to where we need to be.

Judging Others

Just when you're about to judge a person, stop and remember that that person is being dishonest with him or herself. They are so far afield from their purpose that all you can do is give them a little nudge, hoping they'll turn around and get back on track. They're simply unaware of the power that resides within them.

By "simply unaware," I mean that these "lost souls" have tuned out their IGPS so long ago that they are operating on their own conscious "steam," tangled in the idea of themselves as driver. Sometimes they just need to be reminded that Source is "The Father," and they don't have to feel so lost and abandoned because, in fact, they are not lost, abandoned, or disconnected.

When people feel so lost, they seek out every way possible to find their way and get back on track. That's why it behooves us all to help a friend or even a foe when they most need somebody. That's why we are born into families—so there is always someone to whisper a word or two of encouragement to get us back on track when we know we are straying. Even a total stranger could step forward and be of that service to us.

It's just as if you'd adopted a child. You've been chosen to be that child's guardian angel. Also like that child, all of us are connected to Source. Maybe it takes you to be that child's voice and help him find his purpose, and especially let him know that all power lies within. We are all made of the same stuff and have come from the same Source. That's why we can love each other. That's why we can accept another person into our lives with open arms. All share the very same life, and that life is of the Source.

Insecurity within the Self

Sometimes we feel trapped, trying to live our lives based on the expectations of others. We sometimes marry into an overall falsehood, based on our own perception, and we find ourselves unhappy and unfulfilled. We may find ourselves catering to the needs of the person we married (under the false pretenses of who we tried to be) in hopes of winning their love and affection. Having sacrificed our true authentic self for a mask of false self, what results is insecurity within the self.

A false existence has neither substance nor creative energy. When you aren't yourself and cannot comfortably be yourself, you develop resistance within yourself. This built-up resistance can result in unfortunate changes in your health and physical appearance, and within your attitude toward yourself and others. Your physical exterior can suffer, making you look old before your time. Your weight can significantly shoot up or drastically plummet, depending on how you respond to the self-induced stress. Your attitude can become very radical and inconsistent. When you are displeased within yourself, you come to see that nothing pleases you—no thing and no person can displace the displeasure within you. Things and people can seemingly provide pleasure and security, but really, that is just a fear of being alone and a deep state of insecurity. When someone uses another person as a source of "supply," the "user" is simply manipulating and controlling that other person to reinforce their self-pity.

Insecurity is such an all-pervasive force that when it takes over a person, it can be so deep within the core that the entire body suffers. Through it all, Source will try to connect with you to tell you that something is very wrong, and when you look in the mirror you see someone who is very unfamiliar to you.

To get beyond insecurity you have to take ownership of these self-destructive thoughts and behaviors. Simply recognizing the excessive uncertainty that you are trying to mask goes a long way toward resolving those anxieties.

6

Clarity

Clarity can appear just as easily in disappointment as in enlightenment. Letting go of control over others can bring about clarification of situations and circumstances. Life brings clarity through all of the experiences we encounter along the way.

So many of us are afraid of clarity; we are afraid to face the truth when it presents itself. Sometimes the truth will appear in the form of people disliking you, or the feeling that you are not as important to some people as they are to you. If you are so sensitive that you are hurt by people not speaking to you after you've said hello to them in an elevator, just remember that you spoke from your heart and that reciprocation is a bonus. However, if you are deeply troubled by them not responding to you in the elevator, you may also find that your greeting was offered more from ego than from your heart.

Clarity can be your freedom ticket because it shines light on the truth from all angles. It is the mind that controls the self. However, the mind, at times, fights with the soul for the self. The soul fights to be recognized as the Supreme Being that it is. No matter how hard the mind tries, it can never see what the soul sees of you because every soul is different and every mind has different needs. Everyone is already of the utmost presence of themselves, but the mind cannot see this.

Clarity can also shed light on disappointment, especially when it comes as rejection by someone you really care about. It also shows that you are a unique individual, and honors that difference within yourself.

All you need to be is yourself. Do not change who you are for someone else. Change your relationship with that person instead! Get them out of your circle and continue being yourself. Changing for someone will spawn resentment for everyone involved. Allow yourself to be freed by clarity. ("The truth shall set you free.") It is far better to be certain and clear about what's going on in your life than to turn a blind eye to your own existence. So many women get trapped in unfulfilling relationships because they fail to see, or choose not to see, that their mate is cheating on them. Of course, if cheating is an acceptable behavior in your "open" relationship, then it's not a big thing to you. However, that's not the case for me and for many other women that I know. To us, cheating is simply unacceptable. When you allow someone to mistreat you and violate your mind, body, and soul—whether it's an accepted behavior or not—that feeling is damaging and hurtful to you. Whether you admit it or not, or realize it or not, when someone mistreats you or even just takes you for granted, that takes away from your good energy.

Many women suspect their mate of cheating, or even see evidence of it, but because they want to avoid clarity, and believe that "the truth hurts," they wallow in self-pity, creating tensions for all involved. It is far better to abide in clarity, even if it hurts your feelings. The only thing that can be done with hurt emotions is for them to be squarely faced, passed through, and then healed. So expose your pain and confront your tensions so that you can move on to the healing process.

We all have emotional baggage that we drag around. Start to unload it right away! Allow yourself to go through the healing process. Start by speaking it out loud and writing it down, and discovering what other steps you need to take. It could be professional help, prayer, counseling, and/or rehabilitation. Whatever it is, seek to get it healed. Attend to those feelings and issues so you can move on in your life.

Self-Talk

So much of our disconnection from ourselves comes from our own self-talk. So stop putting yourself down and start lifting yourself up! There are so many people out there who are just waiting to put you down! Don't contribute to their negation of you by indulging in negative self-talk. Encourage yourself when you need to, step in and *be that helping hand to yourself.* Give yourself the attention and the love that you seek and deserve.

One method of gaining a deeper appreciation for yourself and transforming those negative energies into life-affirming energies, is through appreciation exercises. Every day for a week, set aside a little time to jot down why you appreciate yourself. Take the opportunity now to start by thinking about your finer qualities, and whatever it is in you that strengthens your commitment to yourself and to others. Right now I want you to think—*I appreciate the fact that I am!*

The person you're changing and working on is you. By looking at yourself in a wholly positive light, you'll be encouraged to look within and find the qualities that you value most. With faith in those qualities, you'll be able to build the life of your choosing.

For example: I appreciate the fact that I am courageous. Of course, what is stimulating to a physically courageous person—say, a rollercoaster ride in a theme park—may mean little to the person who is courageous in an interpersonal sense—unafraid to speak up and act, as needed. Courage to engage in life is called for in practically every moment. I like to think my courage comes into play all the time!

Another example: I appreciate the fact that I am very curious about the universe. To curious-about-the universe persons such as I, gratification and self-affirmation would be experienced from going to a library and immersing themselves in, say, its planetarium or butterfly room.

Another example: I appreciate the fact that I am exceptionally loving. If you too see yourself in this light, show yourself how loving you can be—first to yourself and then to something or someone else. If you're a gardener, and you're also a loving person, care for your garden all the more! Show your flowers and vegetables the love that you have for them. You might even want to speak to them! Studies show that, like people, they always respond! If you have love to give, give it to the many charities that seek out people who wish to love those less fortunate. You might also seek ways to show love to your next-door neighbor, or your "wayward" brother!

Your actions are not defined by how others are responding to your self-appreciation. So find out why you appreciate yourself so that you can learn what mentally simulates you and helps you to grow. If you wait for someone else to appreciate you for what you have to offer, you are giving that person the power to determine what mentally simulates you, and what defines you. Know that no one can determine better than you who you are and what thrills you.

In the long run, it is far better to be clear and certain about where you are in your life than to be confused and uncertain about your circumstances and situations. Take pride in your clarity and let things be the way they are. Things are the way they are! (In other words, "It is as it is.") Don't think things can be other than the way they are just because you choose to be unclear and distort what is. Being confused is a choice that we make.

Take full responsibility for your own clarity by understanding and accepting facts to mean what they mean. Go through pain if you must, but quickly move beyond it to the healing process and gain clarity in your life for your own sake.

Lastly, being clear with yourself about things doesn't mean that clarity is expected or required of anyone other than yourself. You have no control over anyone else, but you do have absolute control over your own thoughts and emotions. Let people be who they need to be, for it is their birthright. All have their own destinies, and live the life that they choose. With unblinking clarity, do what is best for yourself, and make choices accordingly.

Unreality

So many of us want to exist in unreality because we are afraid of rejection; we are afraid of being ourselves because we want the approval of someone else who would have us be other than the way we are. It's so much easier to turn a blind eye and keep our mouths shut and stay in this frightened limbo.

Have you ever asked yourself these questions: Why do I seek the approval of others? Why do I need validation from someone else to know that I am worthy?

Validation is already built into life's design. In order for Source to express in sprit, people have to procreate. Life made us attracted to one another. Most of us instinctively love our babies at first sight. Shouldn't that be enough validation and confirmation that we are loved by others, simply because life has made us that way?

The answer is no! We are not satisfied by the fact that life has made us automatically appealing to our mothers and our mates. Individual consciousness wants more! It wants to feel especially important. Attention is the only thing that feeds into this desire, and consciousness craves it. The thoughts that stream through our minds are often extreme and selfish. If you allow your thoughts to control you, you'll exist in unreality.

A person who lives in unreality (delusion) is one who seeks validation much more than the gratification of mere coupling. Great examples are women who want to take men away from their wives. What has happened to them? What level of insecurity are they experiencing? While insecurity can arise from flawed nurturing and societal influences, it is easy for us to get this way—so lost that we have to seek approval from people when we really should be looking within ourselves to find the greatness ("Kingdom of Heaven") right there!

Insecurity is hard to recover from because we get carried away with the faux freedom and faux excitement we get from our wishful thinking.

Seeking self-acceptance from others stems from not being in connection with our Source and spirit. That's why no matter how much acceptance we get from others, it is never enough because it has no relevance to spirit or Source. Your connection to spirit and Source is vital to fulfillment.

If you are waiting for someone to approve of your personality or your talents or your appearance or your whatever, you know that you are moving farther away from Source. You are going more and more outside of yourself for the wrong type of approval.

Clarity has everything to do with the choices we make. We have to be very conscious and alert on all levels to accept and make sense of the way things are.

So let me tell you a little bit about how things are: you do not control, own, or belong to anyone else. You can only be certain about you. You are ultimately responsible for your own happiness; you have to make the best choices for you, and you have to love yourself in the ways you want to be loved. Time heals most wounds. Time plus space, plus quietness, can calm the mind long enough for you to begin to open to clarity. Clear-seeing doesn't always show you what you want to see, and it can be very hard to accept. We must be willing to accept things as they are, and then release them to the universe. This is the only sure way to experience a continual stream of clarity and less confusion within the self. Accept the way things are! Don't disguise them and make them pretty. If something is ugly, it's ugly—a circumstance, a situation, even the tarnished soul of someone. What you are ultimately going to do about ugliness is entirely up to you.

7

How Special Am I?

You are a co-creator of existence, and that in itself makes you extraordinary. You're ultimately responsible for your own life, and because of that you are special. You are so special that you've been granted the gift to explore your own destiny, and to do so as a human and not as any other mammal or anything else. Being a human offers one of life's best vehicles in which to explore this existence.

As a human you can soar to unlimited heights in your consciousness. Consciousness and its connection to spirit and Source is the bliss of life. We are bodies of energy, generating and disseminating this life-stuff into our universe while also inspiring change for a better future for all who are with us now or will come after we are gone. You are given this body through which to carry out your life's journey. It is imperative that you treat it well, because this body is the only one you will get to sustain your journey and revel in the sheer delight of being a human.

Treat your body as you would a temple, because it's truly your sanctuary. One of the ways you can begin treating your body well is to start with the basics, an inner and outer cleansing. You have to rid your heart of fear and hate, and welcome love and peace, for yourself and for others. You have to keep your physical self in a healthy way so that you can maximize your lifespan, and, especially, the quality of those years.

Physical Self

Because our external covering, our skin, comes into contract with everyday toxins, one of the ways to treat your body right is to maintain good hygiene. Bathe often and, if you like, use fragrances to enhance your natural aromas. Use deodorant to free your underarms of odor. Trim excess hair all over your body so that sweat can't cling to it and foul your temple. Put on clean clothes after every shower, clean and file your nails, wash your hair, clean your navel, behind your ears, and inside your ears frequently, and with care. Brush and floss your teeth day and night; brush your tongue and gums as well.

Drink plenty of water so you can maximize internal cleansing. Eat more of the proper foods and eat the not so healthy food less often. Exercise regularly and feel your heart rate go up; give your heart the excitement that it needs through exercise. Let sweat flow out of your pores and rid your body of toxins.

Wash your hands when you cook, especially when you cook for your family. Wash your hands every time after using the restroom. Cleansing is particularly important after using a public restroom—shared spaces are a stomping ground for bacteria and diseases.

Always wash your hands when you come in from outside. You'll be surprised by how dirty they can get, even if you think you're not touching many surfaces.

Sex! By all means! Have safe and protected sex all the time. This is the twenty-first century, and you can protect yourself by using condoms. In addition to being *fairly* reliable contraceptives, condoms can guard against the many sexually transmitted diseases that continue to plague us. Because we live in a time when premarital sex is commonplace, condoms and birth-control pills are as appropriate for couples in committed relationships as they are for those who are uncommitted, often with multiple partners.

Committed relationship or not, be sure to protect yourself unless you are absolutely certain that the person you're exclusive with is also exclusive with you. Having unprotected sex, especially with someone you're not married to, is no reason to assume that your partner is exclusive with you. Nor is having unprotected sex likely to make that person feel any more committed to you.

Confession

Time and time again, I hear from women who tell me they are using their bodies with men in hopes of inspiring commitment from them. Needless to say, their plans backfire and the men are no closer to being committed or faithful to them. Many women confide that even though they aren't certain as to how committed and devoted their mates are, they still allow these men to come in and out of their lives, and in and out of their bodies. So many times their wishful thinking confers "one and only" status, when in actuality they are one of many. All too often women are in relationships with men who don't consider themselves to be in a relationship with them, or anybody else, for that matter.

It's sadly surprising how many of us fall into the trap of not taking care of ourselves, externally and internally, and who take their precious body, mind, and spirit for granted. So many of us "settle" for relationships that aren't anything other than two people hooking up.

You Are Special

The love and beauty that you are inside behooves you to take excellent care of yourself in every way. Be alert and proactive when it comes to your body. Pay special attention to its needs for rest, fresh air, sunshine, recreation, and good food. Be careful about what you put into your body, and learn all you can about how to take extra good care of it.

If you are going to enjoy this incredible lifetime journey, your bodily vehicle must be healthy. In taking care of your physical you, you begin to regard yourself as special. Growing in awareness of your value, you show yourself how much you appreciate yourself by paying close attention to your health and overall well-being. So work on developing the inside and the outside with the same level of care.

Internal Self

Always go the extra mile and treat yourself very, very well! Talk to yourself in a positive and respectful manner. Treat yourself first-class, and always surprise yourself with delightful, fun, and creative treats. For example, you can take a bubble bath with extra bubbles just for fun. I could go on and on, suggesting ways to treat yourself like a queen or king, but all my thoughts would be subjective and relative to my norms and customs. You alone know what it would take to go that extra mile to treat yourself remarkably. It could be as simple as sitting under an oak tree and giving yourself that well-deserved peace of mind, that break from the hustle of everyday life.

You deserve notable treatment because of what makes you who you are, and that is your soul. A soul like yours is a soul like no other. You have a force within your body that enables you to live and create so that you can carry out your life's mission.

You are the most important thing to yourself, the center of your own universe. You must wake, eat, breathe, think, and love, and that makes you very special. You are exceptional not only because you come from a Higher Source of being, but because you are an essential part of that Higher Source. You are special because you are a body of energy. What you choose to do with your own inner powers is up to you. Your life is a flow of energy with which you can do anything at all.

We Are All Special

Everyone is valuable. The "bum" on the street is as valuable as the most glamorous Oscar winner! You are unlike anyone else presently on Earth, or who has ever lived. We all look different, we all have different personalities, and we all smile and laugh differently.

We need to start looking at people as gifts, for we are all truly gifts from life—*presents of Presence!* Sure, we are all packaged differently (short, tall, big, small, dark, light), but at the end of the day, we are all people. We need to stop judging others by their exterior physical self—a choice not their own—and look at how special they truly are by the soul they have within. After all, we are all just people.

Learn to really see and not judge others, for judging never makes or accurately describes the character of the other individual, or helps him in any way. All it does is highlight the weakness within your own self.

Energy

We are energy beings. We vibrate. We have the active force of spirit within us. We all stream energy. If your energy is used to wreak havoc on others, that destructive energy flows into all the other negative energy that is streaming in the universe. But if, on the other hand, you harvest energies that are loving, your life will stream and flow along with that path of energy, gathering momentum.

You create all that is. The energy that we are streaming throughout the universe is of our own creation. No single person has the volume of destructive mass to activate catastrophe on their own, but enough energy can combine with attracting streams of similar destructive energies to enable just one person to bring about large-scale devastation.

It is possible that disasters happen as a result of the electrical and other subtle charges that are streaming in any one given area, and it is likely that all energy currents don't carry the same charge. So as the energy travels the Earth, the core energies of the planet itself collide and create catastrophes. There are wars, hostilities, and crimes all over the planet creating a particular stream of energy, and as that energy travels the Earth, it collides with the already existing core energies of the planet to create a reaction.

I speak of destruction to let you know that in order for us to create a better world, we must change our energy from negative to positive. It is within our power to foster cosmic changes within the universe.

The fact is, we learn from experience, and experiences cannot be experiences unless they are born of some uncompromising energy. So I speak here about destruction only to emphasize how important we are in the overall scheme of things in this universe.

Calamities are among the hardest events that we have to deal with. We can't understand why a bridge would collapse at rush hour, or why a tsunami would sweep away millions of people, or why a bride would lose her husband at sea on their first fishing trip together, or why an earthquake is responsible for taking 200,000 lives.

Although you as an individual probably have a lot of joy and good wishes for others, and especially for the ones you love, devastating events can and will still happen because of the collective charge that we carry. That energy is expressed in the universe full-force. We have no direct influence over anyone else's energy, but we can inspire one another and foster a better self so that we can begin to manifest universal changes that are in cosmic alignment.

While the love you have for someone is sometimes enough to calm the turmoil within that person, your loved one cannot be controlled by you.

Reinforce Goodness

Whether they know it or not, all people are in control of themselves. So it is important that you acknowledge your specialness—meaning special to yourself—knowing that you are uncommon because you are from Source.

The limits you have set upon yourself are limits that you can just as easily remove. Anything you want you can have, and time is the only factor in this thing called life that moves us forward to what is next in our lives.

Expressing goodness should be natural, for if your stream of energy flows with the good, then good is what your source of energy will embody. When you harbor the destructive energies of fear, hatred, resentment, and unforgiveness, your stream of energy can only express as destruction, whether of bridges and buildings or of lives. At the end of the day we are all people, people with different goals and purposes, but all wanting the very same thing—happiness.

You've been given this lifetime opportunity to truly shine. I can't speak for the people who preceded me, but I do know that all took part in bequeathing the freedoms, comforts, and opportunities of our twenty-first-century lives. Their loving energy has reached from past to present, so that we might have a better today.

We all want the next generation to have a much better experience than we ever did, and it's this hopefulness that streams our well-being into the future, propelling our society to the next level, each and every time.

Technological innovation and advancements over the past 20 years have changed almost everything about how the world functions. During this time it seemed that every year brought major advancements in how we communicate and share information.

The Magnitude of Energy

It is no coincidence that the age of technology is upon us. Advances in technology have burst onto the scene more quickly than expected because our collective consciousness desired these advancements. That pool of progressive energy connected to Source to find the best means to help us along to our co-created destinations.

We can, en masse, project our stream of well-being to benefit the world each and every time around. For example, if we are all consciously or subconsciously communicating with spirit and connecting to Source with the common desire for technological innovation, Source will respond and make the adjustments and speak to spirit to make the necessary changes.

The energies that we put out into the universe are of both conscious and subconscious origin. Consciousness takes on an independent life of its own to connect with Source and manifest the changes we so desperately need in this universe. Consciousness is independent of spirit and independent of us as well. At the various levels of consciousness we can communicate with Source to assist in the progression of self-discovery and self-purpose, but we can also change the world. Life is designed that consciousness is its communicator, informing and inspiring life so that it can be continually shared and moved into well-being.

It is predicted that millions of years from now all the continents will merge into a singular, contiguous supercontinent, "Pangaea Ultima." Perhaps this will be a result of the closeness we are streaming into the universe from our many countries, realizing love and unity for all beings. Consciousness is listening to well-being and is bringing us closer together.

The Internet is truly a masterpiece of life's design. Since it emerged we are able to visit all regions of the globe, and all the great and not-so-great thinkers, without having to leave our dens. For all its very obvious attributes and less obvious flaws, we can all agree that thanks to the World Wide Web, we have become much closer to our neighbors all over the world. The "Global Village" did not exist in the past.

Where Do I Fit In?

Though it can now be accelerated, your progression toward purpose need not reduce the amount of time you have in fulfilling your destiny. This accelerated discovery of self-purpose actually allows you to spend as much time as you like in realizing your life's purpose, instead of spending most of your time just traveling to it. In other words, the quicker you get to the discovery of self-purpose, the more time you have to enjoy your destination. It's like traveling from Canada to the Bahamas, and you initially take a bus. Then let's say the bus breaks down along the way, and you crazily opt to ride a cow across a few states. Sagging and panting under your weight, the poor beast drops dead in New Hampshire, so you plod along on foot, all the way to Connecticut. Wising up, you take a train to Florida, and then a boat to the Bahamas. But despite the swaying palms and margaritas by the pool, you're exhausted, and you can't really enjoy all the hard work that you've put in because you're in pain. Of course, had you simply taken a three-hour flight, you would have had ever so much more time to really enjoy your trip from Canada to the Bahamas.

I use this analogy only to urge you to take the time to do what you've come here to do. Life has given you the opportunity to partake in it, and to create a particular reality for yourself, while also using your energy to realize a perfect world.

Consciousness in the twenty-first century is streaming now, making it easier for us to get to our destination more quickly so we can enjoy our life's purpose fully. It is possible that spirit is recycled and reincarnated to progressive souls. But I am certain that Source collects feedback from spirit so that the next generation co-creates with a better IGPS and more instruments for fulfilling their life's purpose, along with creating a better design for this one.

Life's design is unspeakably sophisticated, so this kind of recycling mechanism wouldn't surprise me because all of life is made up of a stream of well-being. Life itself just wants to get better and be better for its co-creating people. Take a look back and see how far we've come as a generation. We've emerged from the darkness of the Nazi Holocaust and slavery into the light of the Civil Rights Movement, women's rights and much greater openness about sexuality, and technological advances, like computers, high-definition TVs, and hybrid cars. Life has continually transformed itself to fulfill our purposes in co-creation.

Life is definitely a reflection of our mental content and how we live and what we want, on a conscious and subconscious level. As part of life's design we are always connected to Source through spirit. We experience the world through spirit, and spirit is gathered back into Source once we've left our mortal coil.

As the saying goes, "Life is what you make it." Life is indeed what we make it, and for all those who are to follow us.

To understand how special you are, you have to know that you are truly an indispensable part of life, and that life is so perfect that we can experience this perfection.

8

What Should I Be Doing Now?

Life Map

Now is the time for you to get rocking and rolling along in your life's journey. Now is the time to decide what you want and what you don't! Declare that today will be the start of a new you, a better you, a more confident you, a more knowledgeable and prepared you. Now is a good time to pull out your spirit map, or create a new map for your lifelong journey. Your map should be studded with things you want to achieve, and include a feeling map that describes how you want to feel along the way.

Along a typical timeline, for example, you may have listed career, family, and travel. I want to advance in my career to the next level within the first five years; I want to start having children by the time I am 30 years old; and I want to travel to all seven continents by the time I'm ready to retire at age 55. This is a good start for you, but you've got to include how you want to feel along this timeline you've set for yourself.

The solution to life is not just in doing things, but deeply enjoying and rejoicing in what you do. Life is about connecting, and spiritually being a part of the things you've set to accomplish on your journey. So looking at this list again—career, family, and travel—determine how you want to feel during your career, every step of the way. Determine how you want to feel in a marriage. Feel how you want to experience the world. And if your list is different because you're beyond the stages of career, marriage, and travel, then devote your list to spiritual plateaus that you are seeking to attain in this paradise of existence. However, for most of us, career, family, and travel are still the primary foci of our life's journey.

In the career goals section of your map, you may want to write something along the lines of: "I will start in this position and work vigorously but effortlessly, ever increasing in sensitivity and expertise so that I can move to the next level. When I reach that level, I will commend myself for the work I've done, and I will help others along the way. I will carry out this position with penetrating insight and openness to new learning, continuously sharpening the tools I need to move to the next rung. I completely accept that I must expand my sensitivity because it is necessary to the position. I will admit to and correct my mistakes swiftly, and within two years I will be in a position of significant leadership. I will feel empowered and respected, confident that I know my job perfectly. I need to be, and will be, constantly stimulated, and I will creatively guide and complete every project that I'm in charge of running. If I don't feel that I am achieving these goals within three years, and if I don't feel that I am being appreciated in the way I expect to be within the three years, I will not be moved by the lure of 'security,' and will move on."

Proceed in the same way with the family section of your road map. Write down what kind of spouse you want to be and to have, and write down what kind of parent you want to be. Describe how you intend to split duties with your spouse. Write down how you want and expect to feel in this relationship, detailing what is important to you in your life together. Have another section in this area to guide your relationship. It is okay to make commitments and promises to yourself along the way to make sure you are on the right road to your desired relationship. For example, you may want to set the intention, during your first two years of marriage, to remind your mate of how special he is every six months. "I want to bake him a special chocolate cake, symbolic of my commitment to reminding myself of how special he is to me. . . . After ten years of marriage, and as affirmation that I have done the best that I can as his wife, I will travel with my spouse to Egypt. Upon arriving there, all past hurdles will become distant memories. On the trip back, I will rest and reset the clock so that I may enjoy another 10 glorious years with the man that I fell in love with.

You also stated that you want to travel to all seven continents before retiring at 55. So you write down where you want to go and how you expect to get there. In what way will this trip be symbolic to you of having met other goals?

Disconnection along the Way

Any disconnection along the way would indicate that things aren't flowing and going as you would wish, so you may need to make some immediate adjustments. For example, say that you wrote on your map that on or before your 30th birthday you want to open your first restaurant. But as it happened, you lost your leg in a car accident, and you've been set back many months in rehabilitation. During this time, you discovered that you no longer have an interest in food, or in opening a restaurant. So as your 30th birthday approaches, you reassess your life map and remember that you'd wanted to open something big, and do something grand by that time. You ponder long and hard, and finally come up with the idea of completing a triathlon and starting your own organization for disabled athletes. Now it is doors to your new organization, not the restaurant, that you want to see open.

Life inspires us and changes us. Goals change. Things and circumstances change. Laying down stepping stones in your life is a good thing, but sometimes those stones may look different and serve different purposes as a result of life. You have to take and accept life for what it is, no matter what. Not everything you plan for yourself is a part of life's plan for you. What you've decided for yourself may not be what you've come here to do. Life will let you know what you're to do. Just embrace and accept what life is presenting to you, and you'll be surprised to learn that self-fulfillment is prominently featured on that life path. Your revised map may not look anything like the map you've created for yourself, but it is in your best interest, just the same. . . .

Spirit

Your spiritual roadmap is actually a commitment between you and your spirit regardless of what life does. Seemingly without your input, you'll follow the path of feeling good. Now is a good time to reflect on yourself and determine what stream of energy you are flowing with; are you in a positive or negative stream of energy? A foolproof way of determining the nature of your stream is to look at your mental state. Once the vision in your head is clear, you must hold to the choices you've made to support that vision. You have to make choices. And then you have to trust, and not look back, and just go with the flow, knowing that it will lead you to where you need to be. Flow will only go in the direction of where it should, to that vision you have created for yourself.

Positive Attitude

Your attitude is an exact reflection of where you are in your life. Your attitude is a reflection of your heart. Your outlook and attitude about life and others clearly mirror the attitude you have toward yourself. Attitude is everything! Have you encountered someone with a bad attitude lately? Did you also notice how that attitude reflected on them? Doesn't it seem like a dark cloud just hovers over their heads? You almost want to run out of the room when you see them coming, because they are so dark and dense. Most times we don't compare ourselves to those people. We may instead admit to something along the lines of: *I know I have a bad attitude, but you have to cross me to see that side of me.* Yet it is precisely that side of you, your own dark cloud, however well concealed, that you need to address immediately! It's the only way to help you forward in developing a better attitude. Everybody knows it's not appealing to have a bad attitude. So why would anyone consciously harbor such negativity, waiting to pop out at the slightest provocation? Why do we give people the power to make us mad? It's because of our own expectations—what we expect of others. Such limiting factors bring about the misfortunes that we create in our lives.

A positive state would look like this: You are generally happy and things always seem to go your way, and you smile more often than you frown throughout the day. On the other hand, a negative flow would look like this: Your thoughts are mainly negative; you are frequently battling people; you are mostly in turmoil and you don't have a caring attitude toward life. You just take each day as it comes, frowning your way throughout the day. Your presence does not inspire, or bring joy.

When I describe a positive versus a negative mental state, I am talking about the amount of time you spend in that emotional state. Do you have more positive days than negative days, or do you have more negative days than positive days?

Determine which stream of energy you are flowing in, and strive to live in a more positive stream. Developing a better attitude toward yourself and toward life is no easy task. You've been stuck in negative conditioning for so long! The resulting pessimistic expectations can be our worst enemies. They limit or totally block our awareness of the joy in the here and now.

How many of us can honestly admit that our attitudes are a little shady—even "out of hand" at times? If you aren't watchful, they can become very negative and loaded with unrealistic expectations. I remember one time in particular when I boldly cornered my attitude in a tight space, to really check it and confront it. To begin to welcome change into my heart, for myself and for others, I went out and purchased audio recordings of positive reflections and affirmations. And what I discovered is that it's not easy to heal your heart of all the pain it's endured, but over time you can make a difference. Loving yourself can only result in love for others. Over time, you can even come to genuinely rejoice in their joy, as if it were your own.

To foster change within yourself right now is to start with gratitude. Develop that grateful attitude, mindful of all the people, things, and circumstances that you are grateful for. Doing so will open up the doors within your souls, to share in appreciation and grace.

After gratitude comes practice. We have to practice softening our hearts. We have to stop being jealous of our friends, we have to stop being duplicitous, we have to stop worrying about what others possess and are thinking and doing. We have to let go of the pain and the burdens that we lug around. We must banish the bad attitudes and the criticism that seem so much a part of us. We are called to practice peace, love, grace, patience, and hope. It's not going to be easy, but holding to these ideals goes a long way toward creating an inner shift within our hearts, one that makes us a beneficent presence in the world. After you begin to practice a new attitude, a profound inner shift does indeed take place, and you begin to experience harmony. You begin to experience real joy—not just excitement and entertainment. Life begins to change, and so does your outlook—very much for the better. Joy awaits you on this path! But it is not as easy as you may think. You have to work at being centered, as selfless as you can be, as in touch with your soul, and as accepting of the here and now. This profound shift, this fresh new way of living and being, comes about from practice, including meditation, gratitude journaling, selfless acts, and a positive, trusting attitude. This new orientation may take years to establish, as we have been viewing life wrongly, through the limited and distorted expectations that we've imposed on ourselves for years.

Even if you're mostly in a positive stream of energy, aim to increase that flow so you can welcome still more joy and beauty into your life.

The Goal

Determine what and where you want to be in your life and the quality of the energy stream that works best for you. Understand and always be mindful that energy collects and connects with the core of our planet, and that destruction and catastrophe can happen at any time.

Even if you are a good person or an innocent child, bad things can happen. Live your life according to what makes you happy, and not by what makes you frightened, self-doubting, or sad. Live to be happy, to smile, to laugh, to be in a comfortable state of well-being. Although not all of us seem to want to live this way, just consider this for now as a way that you can try.

Open up your understanding of your relationship to the world, and try to sense where you are in the grand scheme of things. That you have this book in your hands right now means that you want more out of life. You probably seek a more developed, controlled, and positive flow of energy in your life. It's time to begin cleansing—mentally, physically, and environmentally.

Cleansing Mentally

A mental cleanse involves clarifying and purifying your thoughts. You want to get away from habitual, negative self-talk. You want to stop judging others, as you can never see or understand the full picture of what has made them as they are. The injunction to "live and let live" is clearly understood and honored. You need to make a conscious effort to be kinder, more self-reliant, self-aware, and self-fulfilled.

Meditation is a great way to quiet the mind. It is in relieving the mind of chatter that you begin to actually relax. And you will relax the tensions not only in your mind, but also in your body. It is in quieting the mind that you can give yourself a break from the litany of fears and grievances that occupy you so much of the time. In quieting the mind, you can begin to pay more attention to how you actually feel and actually *are*.

The goal of a mental cleanse is not only to clean up your habitual thoughts, but also to rid the mind of its constant chatter. You can start by finding a quiet location. Close your eyes and try to ignore all the noise of the exterior world, listen for the sound of quietness. Close your eyes and truly listen to the silence. What do you hear? In the discovery of quietness you free your brain from noise. As you listen for the stillness, don't be disturbed by passing thoughts. See them as clouds in the sky and let them pass. Over time, you will hear the vibration that exists within; you will feel it deep in your core. Don't get spooked out by this! Just embrace the transformation. This is the first step in quieting your mind and allows your soul to really feel at peace.

Cleansing Physically

A physical cleanse includes an internal and external cleansing of your physical self. Doing a physical cleanse alongside a mental cleanse facilitates work on a mind and body transformation. In the cleansing of the body you are "preparing the ground" for change to occur. Through a physical cleanse you are gradually opening a pathway between your mind and your soul. You can start with a simple detox. You can fast. You can increase the amount of water that you drink and reflect on your life over a cup of ginger tea, green tea, or any kind of tea that supports internal cleansing.

An important part of a physical cleanse includes regular exercise. Exercise gets your blood pumping and oxygen flowing through your body. Deep breathing is essential to physical cleansing. Take at least five deep breaths a day—or whenever you think of it—to release the tensions in your body.

Changing the way you dress is also helpful in a physical cleanse. Wear garments that lift your spirits and promote comfort. Overly tight clothes restrict your blood flow and make you feel both physically and psychologically uncomfortable; they can even cause you physical pain. Wear clothes that fit your frame and, in particular, your waistline.

Cleansing Environmentally

An environmental cleanse involves cleaning out your living space and appointing that space to reflect you. You can begin by throwing away old papers, broken dishes, broken furniture, and all broken appliances. Face it: Those old irons and vacuum cleaners cannot be resuscitated! Clean out and dust your living area. Sweep and vacuum under beds, under stands, and under tables. See that your living area is both comfortable and stimulating, so that it is wholly pleasing and relaxing to you. Surround yourself with images and objects that inspire or comfort you.

For instance, you may want to paint your bedroom light green because it's your favorite color. You may want to frame an image of a rock, and hang it in the center of your bedroom wall to remind yourself of your strength and determination. You may want to immerse your bedroom in candles and essential oils that can help you relax and put you to sleep. A plant in your living room, given good sunlight and the right amount of water, can be symbolic of yourself. Let its vitality be a representation of you, but for that plant to thrive, you must nurture it.

A change in your surroundings can deepen the connection between yourself and your soul. Whatever you do, let it help prepare you to participate in a rewarding journey and an embrace of each moment.

Moving on in My Life

You must also rid yourself of people who aren't benefiting you on this journey of life. As you progress to the next level of your life, you may need to leave behind something or someone, or even your own "old ways" that once served you well. Most of this movement will take you in the direction of new territory. Movement inspires new emotions, and opens up a new mental, physical, and spiritual space that you aren't familiar with.

Now's the time to blast out of your comfort zone. We are so used to being comfortable that we don't know what it feels like to broaden our horizons. Moving on will always open up new and more expansive vistas.

The question, of course, is *how?* How can I keep my eyes focused on the unknown without looking back or returning to how things used to be or to what I already know? The way you do that is simple. Or at least I can say it simply: *You have to look forward and trust.* There is no easy formula for leaving behind old habits and relationships so that you may find your way to new experiences and to the next level. But whatever you do, make sure that it complements you and works for you. Acting and reacting out of fear gets you nowhere. You have to base your actions on trust. You have to trust that all will be the way it should be. And why should trust be your lodestar? Because life has given you all the intelligence you need to live, all the breath and nutriment you need to sustain life, and all the insight to steer a clear and satisfying course. As with breathing, you don't have to think about it—it just happens. That's what the proverbial "leap of faith" is all about. We can leap without fear of crashing and burning because we are jumping into a gracious and supportive universe.

So what can you do now to get the strength to move on? What can you do *right now?* You can be clear in the vision you have in your head about where you see yourself. You can develop and take some time to nurture that vision in your head. It may not seem all that significant—it may even sound like engaging in pipedreams—but you have to accept one fundamental fact: It is that vision that changes our lives! It is that vision we hold of ourselves that conjures the people and places lying just around the bend.

People move in and out of our lives all the time. We have to decide who we'll keep and who must be let go. We are the ones to control the stream of energy that we are aligning with. Our deliberate and conscious efforts can refine this energy. When the people in our lives work for us and with us, we are going to smile more often; we are going to laugh more often; there will be no doubt or question marks about our relationship with these people.

Acceptance of People

Acceptance is the solution to understanding the people in our lives. We must accept the role that these people are playing, and the unique way they're playing it. People can serve as teachers; so many people come into our lives just to teach us something. We actually, in a sense, dream these people into our well-being, and they come to teach us something.

They may come into our lives to teach us how to be resilient, humble, loving, accepting, caring, tough, and or even rigid. Sometimes people serve to show us that we have options. Some people act as angels. People are just people, though. No matter what role they have come into our lives to play, they are still people, and people are imperfect. They can be unkind, unforgiving, self-centered, and generally obnoxious. So can we!

Our expectations often get in the way of relating to other people. It is our expectations that distort relationships into inauthentic playacting, wherein no one can tell the true from the false.

We must accept people exactly as they are when they come into our lives—accept that they are who they say they are. Never try to manipulate how things should be between you and others to conform to your selfish requirements. An added benefit from accepting things as they are, is that you change on a physical level, whether you know it or not. Your entire being responds well to your acceptance, and it is through that relaxed and happy response that clarity is possible and the antidotes to your questions become apparent.

9

Why Am I Here?

Most of us ask this question! It can seem impossible to "get a handle" on why you are here when so much seems confusing in life. That you are reading this book suggests that this is one of the questions you are asking. Of course, the deeper question may be: *What is my purpose in being here?* What should I be doing to become more attuned to myself and to other humans so that my life's meaning becomes clear? Asking the universe why you're here is an appropriate question. Ask. You'll be surprised to hear the universe respond.

Take ownership and pride in the response that you get. The inspiration from an answered "Why am I here?" inquiry can only set you off on a meaningful path. Life will let you know if you're on the right path or not. Always go with your intuition. When life needs to communicate with you about what you're doing, intuition always responds with a feeling that is positive or negative. Always go with the positive, and be mindful and wary of the negatives. Negatives are always followed by a continued bad outcome, so spare yourself the trouble and stop yourself from going any farther.

There is so much life to live that pondering just why you are here shouldn't be a primary focus. Don't get caught up in trying to figure out the many whys and wherefores and miss out on all that life has to offer. Only one thing—aside from taxes—is certain in this life, and that is that one day we are here, and the next day we are gone. Life can end before we have even begun to live. Regardless of one's age, the only way to truly live before we die is to keep our minds and hearts open to new possibilities. If you cannot envision something new, nothing new will take place, so embrace difference and change so that new experiences can become an ongoing feature of your existence.

You are here because you want to be. Despite the difficult circumstances that may have surrounded your childhood, you've overcome the stumbling blocks of your innocent youth and have gained a strong character. You couldn't be who you are today if you hadn't had those life experiences.

It is undeniable that the hard times you've gone through have prepared you for most of the challenges that have come into your life. It is not blindly that your spirit is guiding you. It is not an accident that you are internally plugged into the design of life through your spirit. I too have experienced devastation and heartbreak—all to learn what my purpose is in this life.

But just because we are plugged in to life doesn't mean that our journey will be perfect. You are plugged in to life so you can get to your destination as planned. Now you are part of this life. Whether you know what your purpose is or not, that is not the important part. It is vital, however, that you know and accept that you do have a purpose.

If you don't know what your purpose is—by which I mean, if you cannot connect within yourself to understand why you are here—let's do a few exercises to help you get to where you need to be.

Spend some time doing the things that you enjoy doing. If you enjoy cooking, spend more time cooking. If you enjoy hiking, find some trails and head out on a hike. So much time wasted saying what we *would like to do* rather than doing what we'd really like to be doing! Stop and ask yourself what happens to you when you take time to do the things you enjoy?

Most times, you find that doing the things you like or love puts you in a more jovial mood. Why wouldn't you want to devote more time to doing what you enjoy doing? It should be simple enough to do what you like to do, but because so many of us never "find the time," we are left more or less estranged from spirit.

I like going to the movies, so I spend most Sunday mornings catching a matinee. I don't wait to go with my friends, or wait for the person who I am in a relationship with to take me. Although I love going to the movies with my friends and family, I am not going to delay my own joy to wait on them. I simply honor the fact that I like spending that time with myself. I love catching movies to see what's going on in the creative world. All the movies I go to see may not be the best movies in the world, but I am not going to get hung up on that. All I know is that, enticed by reviews and ads, I wanted to see that particular movie, and so I did. Whether I enjoy the movie or not, at least I am doing something that I want to do.

Part of understanding why you are here is to learn what makes you feel good. And the more you keep doing what feels good, the more you figure out what you are here to do.

You may be wondering, what does going to the movies do for me? How does that tie into my purpose for being here? While this book is not about me, but rather about you, I would simply say that the path I am on requires me to be independent; it requires me to get a firm hold of where I am in my life and to have a clear understanding of myself so that I can share my beliefs about life journeys with others. I go to the movies not only because I enjoy going, but because I am strengthening my core. I am feeding that independent being that is so much a part of who I am. By going to a movie by myself on a Sunday morning, I become more connected to Source, and the more I explore and indulge in the things I enjoy doing, the more life responds to me in a positive way.

You may be wondering: If someone is a bad person who actually enjoys being mean, will they be able to find self- fulfillment? After all, it seems that they are pursuing what feels good to them. And I would simply say *no*. Planning to be bad, or even being spontaneously bad, is not a part of life's design. I don't think it is a decision that someone makes to come to Earth to be cruel. I don't think a murderer's co-created destiny is to be a murderer.

Maybe life is not designed to be a bowl of cherries, but it certainly is great for every one of us. It does all it can to work in our favor, inspiring us to realize our purpose as it guides us on our journey. When a person becomes a killer, or even just a hurter, it means that they have somehow, because of discord in their backgrounds and consequent disconnection from Source, gotten lost in their lives. Their entire way of being begins to spiral out of control, away from empathic connection with others and into the isolation of unchecked ego. But life has its ways of helping that person get back on track to a better connection and sense of well-being.

One may ask: What if an innocent person is unjustly accused and incarcerated for a crime he didn't commit?

The reason I am continuing to explain your purpose for being here in such an extreme way is that these are actual questions that you really ask yourself. And what about the victim who is falsely incarcerated? You may ask: What is his or her purpose in life? And while I wouldn't know their predetermined mission, I can only know that it is all part of their design.

Maybe they came here to learn more about themselves, and the only way to do so is through injustice. I could speculate about various other possibilities as to why people are in prison, but I will never know that part of their co-created design.

Co-creation is a very personal thing. It is what you signed up for before you came into existence. And while it's easy to ponder the life design of everyone else, it is much harder for us to understand why we ourselves are here. I suggest you don't spend another minute trying to figure out why the murderer is a murderer, or why he goes scot-free while the innocent man is incarcerated. There are, of course, people whose destiny is to serve as advocates for such victims. These beneficent champions of life's intricate design help to free the innocent.

So keep doing what you enjoy doing. It is all part of the journey you set yourself up for. A way to know if you really enjoy doing something is to ask yourself whether you feel free when you're doing it. You should smile continually. You should feel comfortable, and what you do should feel natural. One good way to gauge whether you're in connection with your job or any activity at all is to notice if it makes you feel scared, bored, or uneasy. Are your actions and behaviors forced, or do they flow naturally? That's pretty much all you need to know.

10

Who Am I?

You are a creation from God and of God. You are destined to remain a part of this human race. You are special. No one can be you. You are the only one of your kind. You think your own way, you act your own way, you love your own way. Be your own way! It is okay to think the way you do. It is okay to cry, smile, laugh, and be who you are. So much of our life can be drained and distorted by people trying to control us and inhibit us from being who we truly are. Now, I am not suggesting that you ignore advice from someone who loves you and wants to protect you; what I am suggesting is that you be open-minded and objective in weighing what people tell you, and make your own decisions. I strongly believe that people are essential to our sanity and development, and that we all need people in our lives. Try not to isolate yourself so much that you become closed-minded and "set in your ways." Be open and receptive to what people have to say to you, but own the convictions that govern you. Be your own authority, and let your own thoughts determine your actions.

We sometimes give control to others by not thinking and acting on behalf of ourselves. Letting others have that degree of control is always detrimental to you. Many people find it much easier to turn the reins over to someone else to "run them"; it can be much harder to control ourselves and be responsible for what we do. That is why it is important for you to develop a strong sense of who you are! You and you alone must be the keeper of your thoughts and emotions and the master of your destiny.

Have a personal philosophy you can stand by through your life. Write down who you are, so that the next time someone asks you who you are you can say to them exactly who you are. You might write something like this: I am smart, open-minded, physically and mentally strong. I am true to my word and I commit to those whom I love by showing them respect and kindness. I am humble but stubborn and relentless when it comes to injustice. I take pride in my words and thoughts and I will use every opportunity to learn from my mistakes. Sometimes things are out of my control but I will always stay in control of who I am and be that person I've come to be and ought to be.

And while this is just a general statement, I suggest you do this for who you are in every situation at work, in all relationships, and especially who you are in a marriage.

Sometimes in a marriage we lose ourselves because we are hung up and caught up on what the word marriage means.

Marriage

Just a little bit on marriage before we move along, because I know this is a topic that most of us weigh heavily and contemplate. So who are you in a marriage? Be who you always would be, even if you weren't married. If the person you used to be when you were single is someone you no longer want to be, then change that person, never forgetting that that person has led you to where you need to be. You can't run away from your past, but you can move forward in your life. You can't hide from your experiences. Don't dwell on misfortunes but embrace the lessons you've learned.

Being married shouldn't take away from your goals, aspirations, or even your fantasies. If you cannot show your spouse the person you truly are, he or she cannot love you for the person you truly are. Even if you have imperfections, if you're honest with that side of yourself people cannot fault you for being you. Two things can happen when you show people who you are: they can either leave you or love you.

It's far better to show a person who you are right from the start than to pretend to be someone who isn't truly you. That non-you is certain to catch up to you eventually, with disastrous results.

I am an advocate for marriage, and I do believe that a successful marriage calls for selflessness from both parties so that they may see themselves as one. Only true union can protect a relationship from the selfishness that can erode any bond. Being selfless doesn't have to take away from who you are as an individual; in fact, being selfless goes a long way toward showing who you really are!

Selflessness

Let's look at what it means to be truly selfless. To be selfless means to be unselfish. It means not being so preoccupied with one's self that one is threatened by the other's existence. Being selfless in a marriage doesn't mean trading in your soul for that of another, embracing who you are so that you can grow, becoming one with your partner. Learn to lean and be leaned on by your spouse. Let the relationship be equal, expect from your mate what you expect from yourself.

If you always expect your partner to be loving and selfless to you, be that in return. If you expect your partner to be the provider, be a provider too. While you may have come to an agreement about who works and who stays home, that doesn't mean that one person is more of a provider than the other. It just means that the ways in which you provide for each other are different. A husband may agree to go out to work while his wife agrees to stay at home and take care of the kids. While the husband provides financially, the wife provides by being in charge of hearth and home. Does this mean he should never help out in the home? Absolutely not! He should help out at home once in a while, and she should try to add to the family coffers in whichever way she can. Even something as seemingly trivial as cutting coupons from the newspaper, or calling their credit-card company for a lower interest rate can make a contribution. When you have to compromise too much in a relationship, it indicates that one or both parties are being selfish, and that a disconnection may be imminent.

Disconnection in a Relationship

When your connection feels like it's weakening, acknowledgment of the problem can be used to bring you and your partner closer together or farther apart. Be encouraged by the fact that life is intricately designed for our greater good; it's designed so that we may fulfill our purposes. A relationship that isn't enhancing you or supporting your purpose in life isn't one you should be a part of. Life is so much your champion that it will change your circumstances to facilitate growth.

You are so connected to your spirit and spiritual design that you don't have to worry about a "failed" relationship; in all actuality, that too is a part of the design. That relationship was needed to get you to where you need to be. Of course, where you need to be is relevant to you and to you alone.

I started this section by saying that you are a creation from God and of God. I choose to use the word God here to emphasize that you are from the divinity of life—you are of that, and that is life in itself. Why? Because spirit lives in you.

When we think of God, many of us think of someone or some force so big that we don't question what it means when someone says God. We don't understand God, but we seem to have a common understanding of what we mean by God. So to recognize that you are from the biggest of all big things like God, from the infinite and fathomless, you can begin to understand how amazing you are.

Some people believe that there are people living inside of them. You know how sometimes you sit and talk to yourself, maybe about your appearance, or your reaction to a certain situation, or even just joke with yourself? Well, I know some people who actually believe that they are talking to people living inside of them! In any case, I just think that "those people" are also a part of life's ingenious design. The spirit within us is a little piece of God or life that is given to guide us to the fulfillment of our purpose; the spirit is what connects us to that greater co-creating Source that invited us to live and express our unique individuality. Just as the spirit is a part of life's design, so are those "people" who live within us. You may know these voices as different levels of consciousness.

While it seems unlikely that there are people living within us, I do think that the Source that our spirit is connected to—and that gives us consciousness—is always in communication with our spirit. This is how our spirit unerringly knows how to guide us through our life experiences, giving us what is needed to fulfill our purpose. Consciousness is the communication between us and spirit. It's just how life is designed.

Why are you, you and not a tree? I don't know if a tree has ever been tested for having a spirit, but I know a tree can grow very big and can be very strong and can live a very long time. Trees stem from spirit. A tree comes here to be a tree. A tree co-created itself to carry out its life purpose. Maybe a tree simply wanted to bear witness to life for hundreds and hundreds of years. But I think that people like you and me wanted more. We wanted to do something. I wanted to write, so I couldn't be anything other than what I came here as, and that was a human. People stem from one particular type of vibration, and trees, elephants, whales—all living things—also stem from different frequencies of energy. We are always connected to Source; we are each a part of life's design. You and I were designed to be a part of the human race.

Sometimes we get so caught up in uncertainty that we try to look and act like someone else. Many of us go to the gym, but don't know the full reason why. All we know is that we want to look like the most attractive varieties of everyone else. Have you actually ever taken a good look around? We all look different, but fundamentally alike. No denying that! We may present in different shades, different textures of hair, but we all look alike. I live in New York City, which is a very crowded place. People only look like ants from atop a skyscraper. I see a group of people getting off the subway and they all just look alike. Everybody starts to look like someone I know, or someone who is familiar to me, but essentially we are one and the same.

I know you're thinking you're no Mariah Carey, no Celine Dion, no Will Smith. Wrong. Those people are made of the very same stuff as you and I. Just because they are in direct connection with their Source and know what they have come here to do doesn't mean that they're different from you and me.

Life is so great that we may be whomever and however we want to be. Of course, we've come here to realize all that we co-created for ourselves. If it's part of your alignment to be a singer, then you'll be a signer. Do you honestly think that back in 100 B.C. people didn't belt out notes like Mariah Carey? I think people were singing long before Mariah Carey was born and I'm positive that when "we"—meaning this generation—have all expired, many others will have picked up Mariah's torch. We have infinite resources to fulfill our destiny. It's just the way life is.

So who are you? What better way to spend your time than being you? Spend as much time learning who you are and what you've come to do. If you're aware of your mission, do just that. Don't delay! Life is so intricately designed that all will fall into place to advance what is to be your mission.

Don't just work out at the gym to be like someone else, or to conform to a cultural ideal of beauty or muscularity. Work out because it's a part of your design. It's a part of what works for your spirit. What's so cool about working out is not just to build rock-solid abs but also to release those feel-good endorphins into your bloodstream and get your heart pumping. And we know that feeling good is a part of life's design. Life says that it's good for you to get moving! Activity is a fundamental part of life's design for you and me because we came here as humans, not as immobile trees. Exercise is a part of our makeup; it's an essential aspect of what makes us human.

So much of how we live is influenced by what people tell us to do. All people come into our life for a particular reason and, whether they help or seemingly hinder, all of their influences are designed to prepare you for your journey. Take what you must, but leave what you must too. You can tell when a person is truly a part of your journey by how attractive they are to you in every way. You may find their personality to be "infectious," "engaging," "sincere," or any number of pleasing superlatives. You have an instant rapport and connection with them. You connect spiritually. You know that he or she is there to influence your journey in a meaningful way.

Also, you know very well when you're uncomfortable around someone. You know when you don't connect with a person's spirit. Most of the time you know for sure right away when you're not connecting. But because they appeared to be nice to you, flattering your ego or being generous with their money, you kept them around. But once you learn that they are no longer a part of your purpose, don't' be afraid to let them go.

Like books, people ("walking books") also come into our lives to help us on our way. Sometimes people help to expose the very ugly side of our outlook, and the ugly side can be that you're rude, have a helpless, blaming attitude, are lazy, racially prejudiced, an intellectual snob—the list goes on. Sometimes we don't like to entertain these unpleasant observations about ourselves. But these people come into our lives to expose our own folly and self-deception so that we might get back on track. We have to confront those delusions and negative behaviors within ourselves; we have to penetrate the turnoffs that people feel for us. Listen when life speaks to you and know this—life is always speaking.

11

What's Next?

Spend some time loving yourself and getting to know the soul that animates your body. Be patient with yourself and expect that this is going to be a gradual process. Knowing who you are and what you've come here to do can take days, years, and even decades. Unfortunately, some people leave before they've even begun to figure it out. Commit today to start to know yourself. No matter what your circumstances may be, you are entitled to follow your bliss. Finding out why you have come is among the most challenging of quests. Don't let this lifetime pass you by without trying to follow what's in your heart.

Our heart and spirit guide us, and that is why there aren't any mistakes. Keep listening to your heart and keep listening to your soul, and the best outcome is sure to follow. So many times we get caught up in fighting ourselves instead of listening to ourselves. Lost and confused from not listening to our heart and not listening to our soul, we are stranded on the shoals of utter confusion.

Let your heart speak freely to you so you can sense what's next, what's to come. Stop spending time second-guessing everything that is happening in your life and in others. The things people do and the reasons they are doing them is simply not your concern. Unless you're a detective or secret agent, stop wasting all that time and energy in trying to figure out what others are up to! To truly know what's next for you, you have to free your mind of all that chatter so you can actually listen to your heart.

What's next for you does not include anything or anyone else. What's next for you is only for *you,* and has nothing to do with anybody else. Let's say you've started cleansing and freeing your mind, body, and soul of the junk of uncertainty and the junk of bad habits; you've begun to quiet your mind and to feel something new about the people in your life. You want to get married but the man you are living with shows no inclination to commit to you in a legal way. You begin to see him now as unnecessary in your life. What's next may be for you to move on to a more rewarding, legally binding relationship.

Having put all the processes in place that I've talked about, your mind should be much quieter and open. Perhaps you'll take a deeper interest in a particular religion or spiritual practice, so that your next step would be to find a suitable venue or group of like-minded people with whom to worship and study.

Trust and believe that in time all that you want to know will come effortlessly to your quiet mind. You'll be able to clarify your thoughts and figure out your various commitments to yourself and to others.

It is easy for me to say: *Just trust, and believe that everything will work out fine,* and it is just as easy for you not to believe it! But if you believe that life will take care of you as it is supposed to, according to the co-created agreement that you signed with life, then it will.

Trust is essential to life. You have to trust in life. Ask yourself these questions: Has life ever let you down (and by this I don't mean if life has made you sad)? Reflecting back on your life, can you honestly say that you have no clue as to why certain things happened? Can you say that those experiences had no effect on your life? I bet you would say that all experiences, even the most unpleasant, taught you a valuable lesson, and that without them you wouldn't be who and where you are today. So I ask again: Has life ever given you a reason not to trust it?

Are you still searching for reasons to find fault with life? Hasn't life given you the mechanisms you need to survive—and even thrive? Life has given you all that it promised you—consciousness, a brain, a spirit, and a direct connection to Source. So what reason do you have not to trust in life? Are you hung up on the details of your household, or what happened to you as a child? Maybe that wasn't part of the plan. There is no need to linger over the rough patches. The fact remains that life has fulfilled its end of the bargain.

I was raised in a single-parent home, but that hasn't given me reason to distrust life or not believe it would work for me. We all have difficult situations in our childhood years, but are old memories that important that you can't see beyond them to get on with fulfilling your destiny? I remember in the eighth grade reading Dr. Benjamin Solomon Carson's biography. I was so inspired by his story that I wanted to become a neurosurgeon.

Dr. Carson was born in Detroit, Michigan, and raised in a single-parent home. His mother, one of 24 children, was a high school dropout. She worked to make ends meet for her family. In addition to all the odds against Benjamin Carson, he also had difficulty in school. However, his mother, Sonya Carson, wanted her son to succeed and she got on him about his studies. Eventually he did very well in school. He graduated with honors from Yale and went on to the University of Michigan Medical School. At age 33, he became professor and Director of Pediatric Neurosurgery at Johns Hopkins Hospital in Baltimore, Maryland.

Move beyond your childhood so you can see the bigger picture of what you're here to do. In time, you'll see the correlation between your childhood and what's to be your destiny. You don't have to move forward on your own. We have institutions that are designed to help people move beyond their emotional and physical distress. This is the twenty-first century! It is okay to get help when you need it. It's not the way it used to be, when getting help—especially emotional help—was considered something of a disgrace. What is important is that you move beyond whatever is blocking your path to fulfilling your destiny. Crucial to this process is self-honesty. It is so important for you to be honest with yourself about where you are in this life, because self honesty is the stepping stones to self awakening. If you can't move beyond childhood and adolescent problems and traumas, the rest of your life cannot fall into place and will be a constant struggle for you. It would be like taking a road that's parallel to your true journey road, where you encounter far more obstacles than you can bear. Before long you discover that you might as well get on the main road to have your experience. So face whatever demons you have within yourself to face. Do so now, and it will set you free.

Trust in life and life will deliver.

12

What Am I Not Getting?

Everybody is entitled to work out their own destiny. Sometimes, though, we get so caught up in a relationship that our life focuses mainly on the "loved one," and what he or she is doing. Let people be! Let your children be who they have come here to be; let your husband be who he has come here to be. You must not become so dependent on someone that your life is seemingly meaningless once they have passed on, or moved on from your being their crutch.

At some point in our lives we begin to have a personal relationship with death. Death takes from us someone whom we love, and through grief and time we come to accept that this person has moved on to the spiritual realm. The harsh reality is that no matter what we do or how much we cry, we have to let go and move on. Letting go is one of the hardest things to do, yet at some point we all have to let go of the people we cling to, either voluntarily or involuntarily, through death.

You need to spend this time focusing on you. You need to spend this time focusing on your wants and your mission to self-fulfillment. This doesn't mean that you have to become selfish in your actions, but rather selfless in your response to the world. Embrace your life and it will embrace you.

Show yourself love, and what will result is you will love yourself more. Protect your body and keep yourself well nourished and clean so you can keep harmful germs and diseases away from your body. Dedicate time to your growth and continual well-being, and you will find that virtue is indeed its own reward. Spend time praying and/or meditating, connecting with your soul, and your soul desires will become increasingly realized.

This journey is about you fulfilling your mission. My hope is that the more I speak of your purpose here—one that *you yourself* have co-created—the more you will begin to feel inspired and, through inspiration, find joy, peace, and happiness. It is through inspiration that you connect most with your soul and find self-fulfillment.

Think about yourself, and make sure you are doing what you are supposed to be doing for yourself. Don't let this life pass you by. Spend some time working on your road map, but get busy traveling! At the end of your journey you don't want to find that you never arrived, and that all the time you spent has yielded nothing more than a pretty map.

Fulfillment is not promised to you, but you are here to co-create in your existence. Make a conscious effort to live happily, and make a conscious effort to stop doing the things that cause you confusion and pain.

When life speaks to you, listen to it. When you get that bad feeling in your heart, follow it, and don't do whatever it is your heart is warning you not to do. At times like this, spirit and Source are having a direct conversation with you. Of course, when life says something is good, listen to that too. When you're certain that you feel good about something, you can be sure that that something is indeed good, and that you should follow and enjoy it. Sometimes you'll be amazed at how wonderful and giving a person can be, and almost have to pinch yourself to be sure that it's real. Don't doubt. If your heart says GO, then embrace their kindness.

It is our convoluted thoughts and habits that sometimes stand in the way of making sense of the good and bad feelings that we have. Don't doubt your own happiness, and never doubt yourself. Don't have so many mind-generated rules and rigid stipulations for your life when all you really need to do is listen to your spirit.

Why do you think you need a checklist for every aspect of how your life should be and look? Those are just the prompts of your insecure mental self.

When you hear people say that somehow you actually want undesirable things in your life, and that everything is a "choice" that you've made, you probably look at them as if they're crazy. Why in the world would you want difficult problems in your life? At first blush, it would seem that these "philosophers" have nothing useful to tell you. But what they're really trying to express is that you are using your mind to prevent yourself from connecting to your spirit. If you would pause for a moment and put aside your lists and expectations, you would actually be able to "hear" the directions that are being spoken to you from spirit.

Take some time to fully accept where you are. For example, if you're trying to lose weight, many recommend that you take out an old pair of jeans that haven't fit in years and aim to reach that size. But what people fail to tell you is that first you have to accept where you are! You have to accept that you weigh 545 pounds—and everything that that enormity entails—so that you can see the situation for exactly what it is. Accept that you are there, filling up two airline seats, your knees aching from the burden, your laptop showing that there are no takers on Match.com . . . and then immediately launch changes that would best work for you.

Make a conscious effort to be the one person who will make the changes that you need. No one else is going to fight your battles for you. If you have to lose 400 pounds because it's not healthy for your body to maintain that weight, and not good for you to be regarded as unattractive, then you "have to do what you have to do!" You have to get the help that you need. You have to be the single generator of effort to make those changes.

You cannot wait for anyone to give you approval to start getting your life right. You have to be that person yourself. You may be saying, "Yeah, that's easy to say when the example is about losing weight." But I must tell you that, regardless of the changes you wish to make, *you* are the only person standing between the struggling you and the fulfilled person you are destined to be. If you're like many single women out there looking for your beloved, what stands in the way of love is none other than you yourself. Ask yourself: *What am I doing or not doing, thinking or not thinking, that's keeping love at bay?* It may seem that every time you look around you see that people are getting married. Yes, they are—they're just not marrying you.

This is the time to see which of your thoughts are going for and against you. Now is the time to determine if you're truly a giving person, ready to love someone else. See if you have any lists of "requirements" that are preventing you from allowing spirit to find that person you're supposed to meet. Your list may say, "Six feet tall and rich—or bust!" But spirit is likely to have other ideas! If you co-created with Source that you wanted a mate, then it will be in the stars for you to have one. You would know deep in your heart if you are to be married or not. You would know if marriage will hinder or support your purpose.

Love feels central to all of us, try not to get too caught up in seeking love on your own when your main intent should be listening to your spirit. In the meantime, keep working on finding and "following your bliss." Keep enjoying the journey of life. You will see that you'll smile more often than frown if you continue to go with the flow of life.

Detach from attachment. That is, detach from being attached to people and things. Spend time trying to merge with spirit, and things will turn around for you. Refrain from attaching to those lists that limit our possibilities. Rigid ideas alert us to the fact that preconceived thoughts are taking control of us.

When you're tenacious in your thoughts, you're showing that the past has a hold on you. Rigidity doesn't mean that you have a good grip on yourself. It shows that you haven't a clue about yourself. But that's not necessarily a bad thing. It's better to know where you are so you can know where you're going. Let me give you an example. Suppose you want a relationship to blossom, but it's just not working out the way you had hoped. You call him after work, but he's been picking up and getting back to you less and less. You're so intent on keeping tabs on your boyfriend's doings and whereabouts that you're not even aware of how rigidly controlling you're being in your thoughts and actions. Give him an opportunity to enjoy leisure in his own way as well, and you may be pleasantly surprised to find that in all that open space, there is ample room for you as well.

13

If I Could Do It Over

I am sure that if we could all relive our lives, we would have some idea of what we would do differently, and just when we would do it. I'm guessing too that most of us, no matter where we are in life, would take the opportunity of doing some things over and even better, the next time. This is because as we get older, we generally gain a better understanding of why we are here and what we have come here to do. The fact remains that there are no do-overs in this existence. You get one shot to make it happen, and how it unfolds is up to you. Yes, discouragement, disadvantages, and setbacks plague all of us, but we all get to start at nonexistence to get it done. We all have the same chances as everyone else. It is up to you in which direction you will turn. No matter where you are, you can make a new beginning. Given your ever maturing perception and understanding of your place in this world, you can start a new life right now. You may not be able to change your name, banish your relatives, or have a complete makeover, but you can take the steps needed to become a better you. As much as we may try to run away from our history, we must acknowledge that our experiences have landed us where we are right now. And from this "home coordinate" we can point ourselves in the direction of our choosing.

You don't need to do it over. You don't need to right your wrongs. Things are the way they are. If you need to apologize to someone, go ahead and do it. Confront the situation so that you can gain clarity, for once you gain clarity you can let it go. For example, if I could do something over again, I would have gone to a different college. I would have gone to a college that had a track team instead of a cross-country team. I prefer running shorter, faster distances to running longer, slower-paced distances. After running a long-distance race, I sometimes like to sprint to the finish line, experiencing the rush that I crave when running faster races. But the reality is that I can't dwell in the past. I have to accept the college I went to. And, come to think of it, one thing is for certain: I'd never trade in the extraordinary friends I made at that school. I know I wouldn't have been a part of New York Road Runners Club, which is mostly distance running, if I hadn't run cross-country in college.

I am sure we all harbor these do-over fantasies—from where we would have lived, to whom we would have married. But you just have to completely accept where you are, and keep moving forward. It's okay to spend a few moments imagining these could-have-been scenarios; their poignancy might even serve to motivate the upcoming generation. Remember the times you would do over, and keep them close to your heart, but also be mindful that they—and you—may not have turned out any better! Just be thankful for where you are *right now,* and who you have become! Too much energy spent in mulling over what could have been obscures the most fundamentally perfect experience of all, and that is your present.

Here are some things to consider before regret can enter in: time waits on no one, so get a grip on your thoughts, allow your spirit to do your talking, and watch yourself along the way to make sure you're still on track.

Time never stops and never looks back, waiting for you to catch up. How you spend your time is up to you and you alone. The expression, "Let bygones be bygones" says it best—let what has happened in the past stay in the past; especially when it comes to relationships in which we aren't sure whether we are coming or going. You simply keep going on with your life. If a partner has left, or wasn't treating you right, chances are they would have kept right on behaving the same way. People don't change overnight, and certainly some people don't change over a lifetime. Accept a person for who they show themselves to be.

Get a grip on your thoughts! Unexplored thoughts and emotions can tie you down to a life of "quiet desperation"—if you let them. Consciousness is the awareness of life, and if you ignore your IGPS long enough, you can become so lost in unconsciousness that you may not be able to recover in time to get back on track to fulfill your purpose. Your thoughts can lead to an awakened inner self, and can get you closer to self-fulfillment. They can also lead to self-degradation, or even destruction—if you don't stop and check yourself.

Allow your spirit to do what it came here to do, which is to serve as your guide. Connected to Source, spirit is in constant communication with it, so pay close, close attention! You don't have to take on the journey of life by yourself! You were given spirit—some call it the Holy Spirit—to comfort and guide you. Whether you believe in God or not, does not alter the fact that spirit is your internal guide. Be still, and ignore the elevator music of your ego. It is only at the still point that you will truly see and hear.

How do you self-check? The same way as when you're driving and glancing at your navigation system. Write down what you like, and see if your feelings match up with your words. Jot down some goals you'd like to achieve and see if you're doing everything possible to realize them. If a relationship is one of those goals, look deep to see if a special relationship fits in with those plans. If so, make the necessary adjustments and watch out for the self-sabotage of rigidity and stubbornness. Flexibility and openness are the way-showers to a selfless, fulfilling relationship. Remember, true union can only be known in selflessness, and selflessness is required for both people involved.

What if you think you're too old to start implementing changes and a new way of life—what should you do then? First and foremost, don't mull over the past! All that has happened in your life has led you to this book. It will help you get back on track and again listening to your spirit. You'll have to admit that if you're much older as you read this book—and you know what I mean by much older—older than the age at which you would like to have been reading this book—you probably allowed yourself to get carried away with your own thinking, your own narrow views. Admit that you've been dishonest with yourself about who you truly are. Then quickly make amends, forgive yourself, and move on. Take some time out to listen to your soul. Get back on track to fulfilling your purpose. It's never too late!

This book can only serve as a reference for you to honor your essence and goals. Again, the first and only step is for you to get honest with yourself. Forget what friends and family may have said to judge you—or even to inflate you, or pander to your vanity. Only you know where you are. The worst thing you could do now is just wait to die. You didn't come into this glorious world to wait to die! You couldn't have co-created a life of wasting time, and with a denouement of just waiting to die. Source would have never enabled you to come into existence if that were to be your fate. The design of life is so intricate, perfect, and infinitely loving and creative that mistakes just don't happen.

If you look around and see that you are far away from where you need to be, the first thing you have to do is turn around. Then head back to where you need to be. I am speaking about literally acting on your dreams! Go to dancing school, singing school, the convent, or wherever you need to be. Act now! Procrastinate no longer!

Accept the consequences of your foolishness. Yes, foolishness—of deciding to disconnect from spirit, and allowing your thoughts to run so rampant that you need to recover. Accept too that what you could have done in your forties, you can't do in your seventies. Don't expect to start training for your first marathon at age 72 (unless you're shooting for the senior division) after you've been relatively inactive for the past fifty years. Accept that you might have to aspire to a mile at a time before you can reach your goal.

I've known many people who have turned their lifestyle around during their later years, and while that didn't always prevent health issues from coming up, I'm sure it reduced the chances of unnecessary health problems.

If no one has had the courage to tell you that you're the only one standing in the way of your own happiness, let me be the first. For all I know, you could even be a grouch! Life doesn't have to be that hard, and the odds aren't "stacked up" against you. Your circumstances needn't limit you. But as long as you're stuck in your ways and can't see beyond your own box, your chances for self-fulfillment are slim. Set aside some time to ask the really tough questions of yourself: What am I being rigidly unyielding, or closed about? What can I do to open up communication with my spirit? Keep in mind that spirit doesn't judge you; all it does is wait for you to accept it as a guide. So forgive yourself for being foolish, and for blaming others for your faults and problems when in fact you're the only one to blame. Why am I so passionate and seemingly harsh about letting you know how it is? Well, because you need to hear it. You may have scared away the people who would tell you the truth. You don't need to be anyone's sad story. You've co-created your own life, and it is up to you to make it unfold in the best possible way.

It's better that somebody be totally honest with you than to watch them shake their heads at you and turn tail. It might be helpful to ask one of your closest and most trusted friends or family members what they've observed about you, and see what they say. Listen, and stifle any impulse to defend your position. If you're looking for honest insights, trusted friends will most likely comply. People are generally adept at finding faults in others, and those closest to you would be less likely to hold back or mince words. But don't look at your faults as negatives.

The only thing you can do once you're fully aware of your shortcomings is to correct them. Faults are roadblocks that you put in place to keep you from getting closer to spirit. For example, if you're arrogant and you know it, can you see beyond the blinders that you're wearing? Can you see that people don't want to be around a person who is so caught up in herself? If you are considered an arrogant person, take a good look around you. Is there anyone around you who really cares about you? And don't say your mother, because your mother will always love you even if you turn out to be a complete creep.

My job is not to sugarcoat anything for you. I am here to be honest with you to get you back on track to where you need to be, and the only way for this to happen is for somebody, or some circumstance, to give you that nudge. Your spirit is just waiting to guide you. There is no need to be stubborn.

14

Accepting Where I Am

Take a deep breath and accept that you are here right now. There is nothing you can do about it. There is nothing you can do about what you've seen growing up. There is nothing you can do about the things people have done to you. There is nothing you can do about the past. Up until now, you've just been trying to figure it out.

It is not accidental or coincidental that this book has come into your hands. There aren't any accidents or mistakes—there are only lessons. How many times you must repeat life's lessons until you get them right is up to you. Millions and millions of people existed long before you, many of whom found themselves exactly where you are right now. Like me, some of them were compelled to write about their experiences, and what they took to be their significance.

What you come to see in all their creations is that everyone experiences uncertainty. And not so surprisingly, our ancestors were uncertain about the very things that you and I are uncertain about—relationships, careers, death, and life. Go back in history to discover and be enlightened by the abundance of people who came before you, and find something you can relate to in them that will give you a feel for what your next move should be.

I am elated to think about the amazing people who have walked this planet. So many brilliant minds preceded us, all brimming over with stunning inspirations and ideas. I would love to have met so many of them! Like you and me, they needed to exist in their own particular milieu, being inspired by the circumstances that would help them to grow. Just to name a few on my turn-back-the-clock "wish list," there is Shakespeare, Newton, Einstein, Socrates, Mozart, van Gogh, and Ben Franklin. Of course, even if we had the choice to live in the time and place of these "greats," not many of us would give up our own circumstances to be with them. Most would not give up their friends and family for anything! So accept where you are now. Accept that you are in this particular time and place for a good reason, and know that you are great.

I doubt that those on my wish list felt that they were great. They didn't walk around knowing that they were going to go down in history as VIPs. They were simply going about their daily business. Did they struggle with uncertainty? You better believe it! They were human, just as you and I are. They desired and dreamed just as we do. We are all made of the same star-stuff, the stuff that makes us dream and live.

Do you think that one hundred years from now you'll be mulling over the circumstances that you are in right now? You would say, absolutely not, because I'll be dead! It follows that accepting where you are now in your life is all that you can do. You can't go backwards or forward in time, but what you can do is create a spirit map from now until the end of your time. You still have time to connect with your spirit.

In fact, you always have that connection to spirit because your spirit lives within you. Your spirit is the essential part of you, everlasting and eternally joyous. The religious teaching about how connecting to your spirit will free you from the woes of life is plainly so. You can become so attuned to your spirit that you "catch the Holy Ghost," as the Christians would say. When you truly abide in the spirit world, you have a feel for what's in you, and must come to the conclusion that something immeasurably bigger than what life appears to be must actually exist.

Another thing religion "gets" is that if you believe and don't put barriers between yourself and your desires, the outcome will be favorable. When wishes come true, it may not always be clear how it has come about, but believing and trusting are always the cause.

Let me reemphasize this critical point: The only thing that stands between you and your blessings is you. And when I use the word blessings here, I am referring to all the things that you desire, and reminding you that only you can stand in the way of your own fulfillment.

What are the steps involved in accepting where you are on your spiritual quest and on your journey through life? To truly accept where you are, you have to let go of the past. Letting go of the past will enable you to drop the burdens that you carry. Let go of the hoary stories you tell of your family life. Let go of who you believe you've come to be. Let go of the constant reference to your past. Let go of all that once was. Box it up and put it in a very private place in your heart. Put it away. Better yet, toss it into a bonfire! When you meet a person for the very first time, they generally don't know anything about you. In fact, they usually accept you just as you are. They don't care to know what happened in your past. They don't care to know why you are the way you are. All they know is that they either like you or they don't. So, whenever an unfamiliar person is looking into your eyes, remember this accepting-you-for-the-way-you-are concept and you won't be so hung up on letting go.

The next step involved in accepting where you are is forgiving yourself. You have to forgive yourself for not being perfect. Forgive yourself for the disconnection you've endured in your romantic relationships and family life. Forgive yourself for being closed to the many inspirations of your spirit. Forgive yourself for the disharmony that you've struggled with all of your life. Forgive yourself for the fight you've been fighting with life. Now is the time to accept that life will always win. You can't fight life and have peace, and you can't fight your spirit, and you can't feel independent from the force that governs you.

The next step toward self-acceptance is not to pretend. Don't pretend to be someone that you're not. Don't pretend to appear a certain way for the praise or simple approval of others. Be real about who you are. Get to know what you like and get to know what you dislike. Do more of what you like and less of what you don't like. When you have to puff yourself up to seem bigger and more important than you believe yourself to be, take a step back and really see what you are doing! At times like these—and we've all had them—you are acting so far out of character that you are experiencing both disconnection and (usually) discomfort. When you find yourself pretending, stop! Remind yourself that it is more than okay to be yourself. If you are not yourself, you are truly nobody! It's okay for you to do things the way you like. For example, in American society, it's impolite to chew with your mouth open. But let's say that, for whatever reason, maybe dental issues, you find it more comfortable to chew with your mouth open. If that's the way you eat, and it's most comfortable to chew with your mouth open, then go ahead and eat that way. Of course, somewhere down the line a dentist can probably solve the problem, but meanwhile—no shame! The same can be said of missing teeth. Ever notice a man or woman placing their hand over their smile to conceal missing teeth?

I am not suggesting that you do anything you like because that is what's most comfortable to you. I am simply urging you to be exactly who you essentially are. Be true to that person, and live a life that's natural to that person. If you like reading in the romance genre and the person you're dating is mainly interested in reading history books, mocking you for wasting your time on romantic fantasies when you should be learning history, tell him to pound sand. A more eloquent response might be no response at all. Continue reading what you like to read and, if you're so inclined, see if you might also enjoy history. If not, not! Something tells me that many of you might still have a problem with the man chewing with his mouth open! That seems very different from someone trying to force their tastes on you. But I would say that both examples are one and the same. It's all about being true to your identity and not capitulating to what others like or what is socially acceptable. It is about you, and you accepting the whole person that you are, warts and all. Perhaps at this point you're throwing up your arms in protest and saying well, how about racists or those with hidden, but very ugly, prejudices? Is it also okay for *them* to be the way they are? Of course it isn't, but they're generally not your business—let their karmic boomerangs strike when the time is right! I am simply saying that you can accept where you are, even though accepting the truth isn't always easy. Nobody said that the truth has to be pretty; in many cases, the truth is a very ugly thing. Situations can be ugly, but there's nothing ugly about who you really are. Situations can be escaped, but you can never escape from yourself.

Accepting where you are is the only way for you to know if this is the way you want to be for the rest of your life. Accepting where you are is the way to inspire and welcome change. It is in accepting where you are that you can begin to see your many challenges. It is in accepting where you are that you begin to work with the truth of yourself, and where you can foster new ideas and changes in your life.

It's like learning to drive a car. When someone thinks he's a bad driver, he goes to driving school. He may even take defensive driving classes and, over time, become a better driver. But everything starts with accepting where you are. You have to accept that you're not a good driver to become a better driver.

Being racially prejudiced is a horrible thing. Yet that ignorance—which may also be seen as soul-sickness—persists, and we still have a very racist society. But it is in recognizing that you have racist attitudes that you begin to welcome change. You begin to see things the way they really are. Having accepted that you suffer from racism, you may meet one particular person from the race you look down upon and actually begin to change your heart just a little bit. But why, you may wonder, am I talking about racism in a self-help book? Because racism plays a huge role in our society, and for me to pretend otherwise, or consider it a taboo subject, would not be being true to myself. And as I said, accepting the truth about where you are isn't always pretty.

I poke at sensitive topics that ordinarily don't appear in self-help books because accepting where you are is all about being honest, and racism weighs heavily on my mind. You can't do this journey of life pretending to be someone that you're not. Being true to yourself is infinitely more rewarding, and is the only way to a better understanding of yourself.

It is in accepting our ugly "truths" that we begin to see that they are actually not truths at all. That which we assume is true of ourselves, and of a negative nature, isn't usually something that we hold as true in our hearts. It is more important to get to know what is in your heart so you can become more of yourself.

Self-discovery is the result of accepting yourself and where you are in life. It is only after accepting your faults and what makes you most uncomfortable about yourself that the pathway opens up to self-discovery.

And while I could give you an example here from my own life, I ask that you reach into your bag of life experiences and pull out one in which you accepted an ugly truth about yourself. My guess is that it most likely led you to self-discovery. Your eyes are now just a little more open to who that person is living inside of you.

I'll close this consideration of self-acceptance with a composite picture of many women I have known: She has struggled with her insecurities and lack of self-confidence; uncertain of who she was for many, many years. Finally, she accepts her confused state for what it is. The courage of squarely seeing where she is then encourages a growing overall confidence. No longer does she linger on her insecurities, and the proof is in her newfound sense of true self.

Self-discovery comes about not only through acceptance of the self but through an ever deepening connection to your inner self.

15

Did My Mission to Earth Succeed?

Another way of posing the above question is to ask yourself: If it were to be all over today, right now, did I complete my mission here? And it is in that reply that you would find direction. We all have different wants and we all have different standards as to what constitutes success. When I talk about success here I am not talking about what you've accomplished and stuck under your belt or hung on your wall. I'm talking about a sense of self-awareness, realized from coming and spending some time here on Earth.

It is so easy to get caught up and lose ourselves, and sometimes we just need a friendly tap on the back, or a knowing glance, to get us back on track. May this book serve as that tap or that glance! It asks you to open your eyes and ask the questions you may be most afraid, ashamed, or embarrassed to ask, for fear that people will judge you.

No one else is manning this Earth "mission" but you. You alone are at the controls, and nobody else is responsible for the choices you make. As a mere spectator, I am here to get a little in your face and remind you, again and again, that you are responsible for the choices you've made. How many of those choices have been, or will be, dictated by others is a choice you'll just have to live with. Meanwhile, the possibility of attracting people who are capable of loving you without requiring you to become something other than what you are, is always present. When you know who you are, those who demand artificiality will no longer be attracted to you, nor you to them. I know I've been guilty of animating this false self as well. Living my life for and through the eyes of someone else to "make them happy" can only result in unhappiness and bitter disappointment—on both sides.

I ask you now to come along with me on a whimsical little venture that I call Mission to Mars.

Mission to Mars

Imagine that you and your family, out of millions upon millions of applicants, have been given the opportunity to go on a mission to Mars—the first family to travel to Mars! Just think about this for a second. You are going into deep space and to an unknown world. You'd likely ask yourself these three questions: What will I take? What do I want to accomplish when I get there? And what would I like to bring back with me? Let's put on our space helmets and thinking caps, and figure out some solutions.

What would you take with you on such a mission? Your list might look something like this: camera, car, shelter, and stuff you need for everyday living. But then you find out that the officials in charge of this expedition will not let you bring anything with you because they know that any unprotected item could not withstand the Martian atmosphere. However, the officials are allowing you to bring along two other people. So you decide to include your spouse and your child.

Now you and your family go through astronaut training for a year to prepare for this very complex mission. Finally the year is complete and you pack your bags, ready to embark on your journey into space.

This leads us to the next question: What would you like to accomplish when you get to Mars? Let's assume you're not a scientist. You're just an ordinary person. Let's say you're a writer like me. You've always been curious about the universe and outer space, but you never really thought about it in any depth. But, you've been given a once-in-a-lifetime opportunity to go to Mars! For goodness' sake, you've been chosen out of millions of people to make a free-of-charge expedition to Mars. You've never doubted for a minute that you want to go.

Since you're not a scientist, you figure the main thing you want to accomplish is to make it there and back safely! Your plan is simply to have a good time and explore the environment.

Prior to the launch you learn that, due to political intrigue, the space program will be shutting down for an indeterminate length of time after this final mission. You are therefore ever so much more grateful that you've been given this tremendous opportunity.

The shuttle launches, the trip is uneventful, and you touch down on the Red Planet. Unfortunately, an asteroid shower prevents you from leaving the space capsule. For a few days you just sit there, looking out the window, increasingly eager to explore this unknown world. You spend those days just hanging out with your family and playing cards. Finally, the asteroid shower subsides enough for you to venture forth. There are no means for getting around, so you have to walk everywhere you go. You sleep just enough and spend most of your time taking soil and rock samples, and photographing the awesome landscapes of Mars. It is now a week into the mission and you've been exploring for only two full days.

As the second week comes around, you get some very troubling news—you learn that the mission must abruptly end, due to mechanical problems.

This brings us to the final question: What would you bring back to Earth with you? Other than the hermetically sealed soil and rocks, you are not allowed to bring anything back with you, because no one knows what extraterrestrial microbes and other oddities might be present, nor their physical effects on humans and the environment. This means that all you can bring back with you are your samples and the memories that are stored in your brain.

As the shuttle gears up to leave, you're saddened at the brevity of the mission. And while you are grateful for all that you've experienced, you, of course, wish there had been more time to see more.

Upon returning to Earth, you see your friends and family members, waiting to greet and congratulate you. You are ecstatic, and can only hope and pray that the space program will be revived, and that your friends' children, and their children's children, might one day enjoy this opportunity.

Life

As we think about how perfect the design of life truly is, we begin to see that living life is almost like going on a mission to Mars. Just as one "gears up" to go to a whole new world, Nature prepares the body within our mother's womb. And just as you were not allowed to take anything with you to Mars, you are certainly not able to bring anything back with you—other than your soul!—into the womb. Except for those sealed rocks, which may be likened to lifetime memories no longer available after death, you cannot leave Mars, or your body, with anything.

Why did you want to go to Mars? Other than the fact that it was a once-in-a-lifetime deal and that you were chosen out of millions, you went simply because you wanted to. It's almost the same with life. One sperm was chosen out of millions to fertilize the egg, creating a house for your soul. Why did you want to come? I guess, as with the Mars expedition, you thought it would probably be fascinating. And what happened on the mission? Almost everything that could go wrong did go wrong; an asteroid storm prevented you from leaving the shuttle for a few days and the trip was shortened.

Finally, when the doors opened, you realized that only one week remained to explore the terrain of Mars. So you woke up early, and spent most of your day awake. You absorbed all that you could. But then you learned of mechanical troubles that would force your immediate return to Earth. You were saddened by the shortened mission, and even more disturbed that you didn't get to do everything that you had planned. The parallel to life is obvious.

You can't control how much time you have here on Earth, but you do know that there are many things you'd like to accomplish. Of course, things just don't go according to plan. On your final day of heading back to Earth, you looked around and took special notice of your family. You'd been so caught up in your mission that you'd all but forgotten them! Having only a few days left to explore Mars can be taken as a metaphor for being "too busy" focusing on your agenda in life to attend to the people you care about most. In "real life," it can go the other way as well! We may indeed look back and regret not having given more of our time and energy to the people we loved. On the other hand, we may also have devoted far *too much* of our energy to others, diverting our attention from the mission at hand. It's all about balance.

Perhaps my make-believe space mission will serve to remind you that you are indeed on a fabulously exciting mission! There is a "world of" things to do and love in this world, and you need to start making plans to dive right in! I also wanted to reemphasize that the mission you undertake in this life is for you and you alone, but that you have to be generous and invite others to enjoy the journey with you. In that sharing, you will appreciate the people in your life and not wait to truly notice them on "the final day."

The design of life is so unique and intricate that you can't help but be amazed. In the lyrics of "Born Free," "Look around you! How it will astound you!" You can't help but ponder whose elaborate design this is. In my Mission to Mars, our adventurers were aware that NASA had orchestrated and funded the project, but the particulars of just how, and to what extent, they (and you) just don't know. We all accept that response. We don't know much about what's going on in the universe, but we do know that something has to be very much "bigger" than we.

And, that bigger-than-we-are thing I am talking about lives inside each one of us. Spirit is the gift that life gave to us upon coming into being. How it got there or why it is there we can't begin to guess. But deep down, you and I both know that the spirit is not something we argue with. The spirit is not something that we dispute. We know that spirit is the very essence of who we are, like the memory of the Mars mission left in the mind of the explorer. Is it God? Is the spirit another word for God? We can only speculate. While no one yet has successfully defined spirit, or God, we do know that if we connect to it and live through it, we will have a more fulfilled life.

16

Here for Me and Not for You

We sometimes get so caught up in a marriage, a relationship, or family life that we forget that we are all here for our own experience. And while we are creatures of emotion, anything anyone else does shouldn't really matter to you. You may be ready to fly off your hinges as I say this, but it is our birthright to live as free spirits until the day we die. When you notice yourself getting too engulfed and caught up in what someone else is doing, take a step back and say—*I am here for my own experience of life*. Nothing anyone else is doing should matter to me. And while you may be a parent or a spouse, release some of that "ownership" of the other person, and let them make the appropriate decisions for themselves, just as you would like to have the same freedom for yourself. Everyone has the privilege and the right to discover the soul within themselves. We are not, after all, just walking around, passively waiting for the day we die. We are all curious about our reason for being and, while we accept that we are all going to die, from time to time this question of purpose does cross our mind. If you are suffering really badly, the question may hang even more heavily, and be expressed more sadly as "What's the point of all this pain?" It doesn't matter what age a person is or where he or she is in their life—we are all concerned about our purpose and our existence here on Earth.

So while a spouse may be busy being the head of household and showing you their armored backbone and their strength, they too are privately thinking about their existence, and what it means for them. Sometimes when the answers aren't clear and there seems to be no purpose at all, people adopt the lowest form of themselves and take an I-don't-care attitude about life. To blot out the pain and uncertainty, many people turn to addictions of all kinds—drugs, sex, overeating, and alcohol—and disregard all commitments they have to themselves and to others. Attempting to black out the harsh realities of their daily existence, they are unwittingly blocking out *all the rest of life,* including its beauty and unlimited opportunity to love and to grow.

You may well ask how you can have a relationship with someone when you and I both know that you are here solely for your own existence, and that nothing anyone else is doing should pull you down or knock you off course. I would say continue working on yourself. Companionship is a natural and necessary part of life. Continue working on yourself, and use that time that you find to check up on your children or your mate to check up on yourself! Make sure that you are gaining clarity, that you are connecting with your spiritual side, and that you are building a relationship with your soul. Make sure that you are following your road map and that you are living in balance. Yes, find the time to check up on yourself! Go through your refrigerator and make sure you are eating the right foods for you. Go through your books and see if there is something that you would like to read or reread. Seek out the joy within yourself and let people live their own lives. When you let people be as they are, they will in turn love you for your consideration. They would love you for taking care of yourself and may even be inspired to do the same, and join you in your quest for self-fulfillment. It's inevitable that sometimes people will want to detach from you and go to seek out something that is missing from their lives. Let them go! Always remember that you are here to live your own life, and what anyone else is doing has absolutely nothing to do with you and shouldn't hinder you.

The best thing that can come of someone leaving you is clarity and, as I discussed earlier, clarity sometimes hurts, but all that's left to do is heal and move on.

You are here to learn, to love, and to grow, to become more of yourself. Don't let the doings or non-doings of anyone take this precious and unlimited experience away from you!

Forgive all the people who have hurt you so that you can carry on with your own life. Forgive people so that you can give your journey the attention that it deserves. You don't want to look back and see that you've traveled miles and haven't accomplished the journey that you've set out to take.

Believe in yourself. If no one else believes in you, be the only believer! Know that you co-created your existence and no one can take that away from you. What you've come here to do, you've come here to do. For example, you don't just go and stand in line at the bank just to stand in line. You go there and get in line so that you can get your transactions taken care of. Let's look at life in this way as well. We don't do things just to do things—we are always driven by a purpose. So why in the world would anyone think they were born just to "kill time?"

What business is it of yours what other people came into existence for? Why is it so important to you what other people are doing with their lives? Do you say it's because you married them, or you brought them into existence? Never mind that. You are your brother's keeper, but only up to a point. Think of it this way: You may want to help a stranded motorist to change her tire, but you'd not linger there all day, psychoanalyzing her! You must know when to move on!

When you detach from all clinging, and focus on yourself, you'll be amazed at what will happen.

You'll appreciate yourself more. You'll love yourself more, and people will gravitate towards you more because you'll be following your IGPS and things will be going the way you always wanted them to go. People will be irresistibly drawn to you because they will feel especially at ease around you. In many ways, it will be like when people are attracted to a happy baby who is gurgling and waving at them. A baby is busy being a baby, and has little interest in what you're doing—the baby simply knows that it's happy being a baby.

It's the same story with dogs. Why do people love being around happy, little pooches and instinctively want to pet them? Because a happy dog is a creature we want to be around. We sense that the dog is happy being itself, and people are attracted to that even if they're not especially fond of dogs. Most people can't resist a cute little dog, frolicking around its owner, no matter what. They just stop and stare.

Do you really need me to tell you the repercussions of being a "busy body?" Well, your being preoccupied with someone else's experience will not get you any closer to your own. Rather, it will keep you at some distance from the Main Event, which is you. It will not bring you fulfillment. You, along with everyone else involved, will be unhappy.

You might say, but Karissa, you don't understand. I love my child and I cannot let him go down the wrong path. I will do everything in my power to see that I get him to be a responsible and productive person in this world. And I would respond that of course you should do what you need to do for your child. But I guarantee that your authority can only go so far before that child rebels. Too much control can only make a child move farther and farther away from you, because the only thing a child wants is to become more of who he's come here to be.

I think parents have a duty to give their children the means they need to successfully encounter and prevail against all of what life has to throw their way. Parents can inspire self-esteem in their children by letting them know, in ever so many ways, that they are good and worthy, smart, funny, and perhaps even cool. Parents have the great privilege of encouraging their children, and rewarding them when they do good things and when they follow their hearts. Parents should also foster creativity and authentic self-expression in their children. But a parent cannot control a child when he is an adult and coming into more and more of himself. A parent, like a teacher or other mentor, is there to encourage a child to do what he has come here to do.

The same holds true of any relationship. I know I've spent enough time talking about relationships, but bear with me as I stress this one last time: It's imperative that we allow people to be who they have come here to be! Don't be a roadblock along anyone's path to self-fulfillment. Keep following *your own shine,* and bask in the joy that you're sure to find—and move from uncertainty to confidence; simply a new way of living your life.

Epilogue

From the Heart

Explore the process of truly letting go, and let people be who they are. Be careful of the company that you keep and make the necessary changes. If you find yourself constantly vexing over the spiritual map of your life, then connect with your Source and your spirit. Just as in day-to-day living you experience road closures and detours, expect the unexpected along the way in your life. Sometimes the sight of construction and repair being done on our city bridges reminds me that the bridges in life will sometimes need repair and construction as well.

Take time to be quiet and still, becoming acquainted with the inner you. Make time and open up space to be honest with yourself about yourself.

Don't devote too much time and energy to learning a single life lesson. Attend to the lesson, yes, but make the necessary decisions to do what you need to do to move forward. Learning and then moving beyond a life lesson is the only way to successfully navigate life's journey.

Spend some time in the past, and spend some time in the future when you want a little escape. But aim to be present, and focus on what you are trying to accomplish here on Earth.

Create a balance on this journey; you need family, friends, a job, and a lifestyle. Balance and give everything love and the full attention that it deserves.

They say that time heals all wounds, and it is true. You need time to heal physical and emotional wounds. You need time to do what time does best, and that is to keep moving forward.

Life is infinitely bigger than what you think it is. Stop fighting over personal opinions and assumptions that keep you in resentment. Don't get hung up on people and what they are doing. Live for yourself and accept that there is a divinity to life that you need to recognize but do not need to understand. So just keep your eyes wide open and stop trying to be Superman.

Be the individual that you are here to be, and be totally honest with yourself, even if not with anyone else. I may have taken you on an emotional rollercoaster in this book, but trust and believe that it was for your own good. I only wanted to stir up some emotions and force a conversation between your consciousness and spirit.

Confronting your demons is the best thing you can do for yourself. You must have a good reading of where you are so that you can know where you're going. Knowing exactly "where you stand," you will not care at all or pay the slightest attention when people attempt to judge you.

People come and go from your life all the time. Some people stay awhile and others just come in and soon they have vanished—seemingly from the face of the Earth. But regardless of how long they're on your radar, people are indispensably useful along the way to self-discovery. Even those who serve to keep you going down the wrong path have an essential role to play in inspiring you to wake up! You have to find it within yourself to be responsible for your own actions. Nobody is better qualified than you to restore your clarity and direction.

Know that spirit is always a patient and loving guide, and that you are never alone in making life decisions. Always, take a minute to ask within, and sooner than later you'll get a response. If you sense resistance and bad feelings that is a sure sign not to go down that path. However, if you look within and you experience a surge of great, self-fulfilling feelings, you know that is probably the better way to go.

You are the co-creator of your life. You did this co-creating a very long time ago. And your existence started long before you were born. From conception onward, you have been conscious and developing a brain with which to understand the consciousness you are experiencing. You've been connected to spirit and Source from the womb. And you know that spirit is an aspect of Source. You recognize that spirit is always a part of you, because it's what gives you life.

Please don't waste another minute. Accept where you are and do what you have to do to get to where you need to go. No more excuses. No more blaming other people or circumstances for your weaknesses and faults. You are responsible for you! Take some time now to own up to your responsibilities. Take full responsibility for your actions, feelings, and thoughts. Take responsibility for being unconscious and lost. If you do, you won't be lost much longer!

This is not the end of your journey. Know that you still have time to make things right. You still have time to do what you have come here to do. You didn't come here just to stand in the breadline and then drop dead. You wouldn't stand around in a queue at the post office just for the heck of it. You would, however, line up to mail a package, buy some stamps, or get a money order. Just as you wouldn't stand around "marking time" in real life, I know that you won't do it in spirit, either.

Do what pleases and inspires you. Don't depend on other people to "make you happy." What somebody else is doing has little bearing on what you are doing. Stop waiting on people to fulfill you—it can't be done! Stop expecting them to go the extra mile for you. Go the extra mile for yourself—you'll feel much better about it in the end. You can't expect anybody to do something for you that you aren't willing to do for yourself. So love yourself unconditionally, and people will love you in the same way that you love yourself. Show yourself kindness, and people will show you kindness.

Respect yourself, and people will have no choice but to respect you. Let that respect extend to every aspect of your life. Be mindfully respectful in the way you talk to yourself. Respect your body. Respect how you live. Have you ever told someone to take their own advice when they were trying to offer it to you? That's the way self-respect works; it's like taking the advice you'd give to somebody else. If you told someone not to eat off the floor because it is disgusting, then you too would not eat off the floor.

I know I didn't discuss karma in this book, but to underscore my point about having respect for yourself, I must include it now. It should be obvious to you that if you don't respect yourself, and respect other people, you've got to expect karma to come back and bite you in the ass. There's just no sugarcoating that basic truth. If you respect your body, you will express that high regard by bathing it, grooming and adorning it, nourishing it, and protecting it from illnesses, nutritional deficiencies, unwanted pregnancies, and careless accidents. Love it, and cherish it with all your heart. If you have respect for committed relationships, don't try to entice someone who is already in a committed relationship. How you treat yourself is how others will treat you. If you devalue yourself, people will treat you as the "no-count" you're projecting.

Who do you think you're truly hurting when you creep around and live dishonestly? You're hurting you the most! You may hurt others who are involved in the situation, but those people usually know that all they have to do is walk away from you. You, however, cannot walk away from yourself. So really, what are you gaining by being dishonest and untrue to yourself? You're gaining nothing, absolutely nothing. If you seek acceptance so desperately from others, you won't get it in the ways in which you truly desire it. At this point, you are blocking yourself off from your own self. I've come across people who are so caught up in their own habits and beliefs, and who are so stubborn, even in the face of their own self- destruction, that all I can do is just shake my head and hope that they get a clue one of these days. I have to accept that there is only so much I can do, or you can do, for someone else. People have to be able to get themselves out of the mess that they get themselves into.

So—do I have it all together? Of course not! Do I deviate from my path and get caught up in my own isolated consciousness at times? The response is yes. I may have better control of my mind now than I did in the past, but from time to time I stumble and fall. I am made of the same stuff as you. So the next time you think you're all alone, know that someone else is going through the very same things that you are. Be open to life, and you'll begin to see the many ways in which all of us struggle. No one is excluded from the woes of life. And because "we are all in this together," we must help one another instead of hindering.

The only thing that happens when you negatively impact someone's life is that you waste your time and energy, moving that much farther away from who you truly are. If your so-called antagonist is following their IGPS, they are going to be good and successful, regardless of what you do or say.

Life is designed to have you continually think about the changes and adjustments that you so often need to make. You have to make changes to get results. *And the time to do so is always now.* If you're not getting what you want, then you must launch the changes that are needed. That's what this book has attempted to inspire. Begin a conversation with yourself. Express your thoughts and feelings on various topics pertaining to what you really want in life, present and future, and take it from there.

Notes

Notes